MIND READING MAGIC TRICKS

BOB LONGE

Sterling Publishing Co., Inc.   New York

STERLING Books by Bob Longe

101 Amazing Card Tricks
Easy Card Tricks
Easy Magic Tricks
Great Card Tricks
Mind Reading Magic Tricks
Nutty Challenges & Zany Dares
World's Best Card Tricks
World's Best Coin Tricks
World's Greatest Card Tricks

Library of Congress Cataloging-in-Publication Data
Longe, Bob, 1928–
    Mind reading magic tricks / Bob Longe.
        p.   cm.
    Includes index.
    ISBN 0-8069-3896-X
    1. Conjuring. 2. Telepathy. I. Title.
    GV1553.L65   1996
    793.8—dc20   95-26204
                                                    CIP

        1   3   5   7   9   10   8   6   4   2

Published by Sterling Publishing Company, Inc.
387 Park Avenue South, New York, N.Y. 10016
© 1996 by Bob Longe
Distributed in Canada by Sterling Publishing
% Canadian Manda Group, One Atlantic Avenue, Suite 105
Toronto, Ontario, Canada M6K 3E7
Distributed in Great Britain and Europe by Cassell PLC
Wellington House, 125 Strand, London WC2R 0BB, England
Distributed in Australia by Capricorn Link (Australia) Pty Ltd.
P.O. Box 6651, Baulkham Hills, Business Centre, NSW 2153, Australia
Manufactured in the United States of America
All rights reserved

Sterling ISBN 0-8069-3896-X

CONTENTS

INTRODUCTION

Although the vast majority of the tricks in this book deal with mind reading, I have included some other types of mental magic. So you will also find here examples of miraculous predictions, strange coincidences, extrasensory perception (ESP), and more.

It seemed logical to categorize most of the tricks by the material being used: money, cards, dice, etc. But included in their own sections are amusing mental tricks (*Fun with Mentalism*) and incredible feats of mental prowess, especially lightning calculation (*Brain Power*).

All the tricks are easy to do; no sleight of hand is used. Still, they are all extremely effective.

TIPS

Variety

Should you present yourself as a mentalist and perform only mental magic tricks? You can if you wish, but I see nothing wrong with presenting all sorts of tricks, including mental magic. In a lengthy routine I will usually throw in several mental tricks, introducing them with a statement like this: "Over the years I've discovered that there are certain phenomena which I simply don't understand. For example . . ." Then I introduce and perform a few mental tricks.

Mystic Forces vs. Natural Means

When you perform mentalism, are you being a charlatan, setting yourself up as some sort of mystic? That is true of some mentalists. But many professional mentalists actually tell audiences that their results are achieved by "natural means." These mentalists certainly don't want to say that they're doing tricks; on the other hand, they don't want to pretend they are receiving supernatural help.

Since I present *all* my tricks in a spirit of fun, there is no question of my actually receiving occult help. Even when I claim that mystic forces are involved, audiences *know* that I'm kidding. On the other hand, isn't it just possible that an effect is brought about through some unusual mental power—telepathy, precognition, whatever? Most spectators are willing to suspend their disbelief so that they can enhance their enjoyment. And the bottom line is this: These mental tricks fool people. Since there is no logical explanation, maybe—just maybe—it *is* mentalism.

Performing

How do you present a mental magic trick? I recommend that you stick with your own personality, just as you do when performing other tricks. Unless you're obviously kidding, don't present yourself as a mysterious creature who has solved the mysteries of the universe. There you stand, with your glaring, hypnotic eyes and your flared nostrils! And there sits the crowd, trying desperately not to laugh out loud.

If you are naturally raucous, stick with it. If you are a quiet person, present these effects with a reserved air, perhaps tossing in a quizzical smile now and again. In either instance I favor taking an attitude of puzzlement. At the end of a mental trick, you are as befuddled as the rest of the group. How did it work? You have no idea; it just *did!* You shrug. Perhaps it *is* mentalism.

The Trick Itself

Whatever your personality, the trick itself must be respected. *Don't* throw it away. The trick is the whole point. Your presentation—including jokes, serious patter, and so on—is frosting; it is intended to augment the trick, not overshadow it.

By the same token, you must choose appropriate tricks. Pick out only the ones that you like and which suit your style of presentation.

Developing Routines

Since many kinds of mental tricks are included here, you can and should include a good variety when presenting a mental magic routine. If you do too many similar tricks, spectators may perceive that you're merely repeating yourself.

Patter

With mental tricks, good patter is important. Suggestions are provided with each trick.

MONEY

Win by a Nose

Since Sam is an obliging young man, you might ask him to assist you. Hold up a coin, saying, "Sam, here's what I'd like you to do. I'll demonstrate." Holding the coin in one of your hands, close both hands into fists. Put your hands behind your back. "After you have the coin behind your back, change it from hand to hand until you feel like stopping. Then bring your hands forward like this."

Bring your fists forward, palm down. Directly facing Sam, extend both arms at full length. "I will try to divine which hand holds the coin."

Hand the coin to Sam. Avert your head as he juggles the coin behind his back. When he extends his arms, you tell him which hand holds the coin—*if all goes well!*

Yes, this is not 100 percent certain. But with the right subject, you can repeat the stunt again and again. If, at the beginning, you should miss, explain that mentalism is an art, not a science, and go into a surefire mental effect.

The secret? When the spectator extends his arms, he should be facing you directly. You look deep into his eyes, trying to fathom his choice. Actually, you are trying to determine if his head is turned slightly to the left or right. Quite often, a spectator will unconsciously point his head in the direction of the hand holding the coin. The indication is *very* slight, however. So how can you tell? Look at the nose! When directly facing the spectator, you can readily tell if the nose is tilted somewhat one way or the other.

Don't pass this up. Usually, it works, and when it does, it's a real baffler.

8

See My Fist?

You will need the aid of three to five spectators. Ask each of them to take out a coin.

"When I turn my back," you explain, "I would like you to take your coin in one hand or the other, and then make two fists and hold your hands like this." Demonstrate by holding your fists at belt level with the palms down. Turn your back and continue: "Now very quietly pick out one person to be the subject of this experiment." Pause. "This is for the person selected: Concentrate on the fist containing your coin. Now hold that fist to your forehead and continue to concentrate. The rest of you, please continue to hold your fists in position."

For about thirty seconds, chat about the mental vibrations you are receiving as you try to read the subject's mind. Then: "I would like the subject to take his fist from his forehead and place it with his other fist."

Turn back to the spectators. Say something like, "I have a fairly good idea of who the subject is." Continue in this vein as you casually glance at the fists. Because the blood has drained somewhat from the fist held up, one person will have one fist paler than the other.

Point to this person. "You are my subject." Touch the paler fist. "And this is the hand holding the coin."

Be sure to add a compliment: "You are extremely telepathic."

A Helping Hand

In the previous two methods, there is an element of uncertainty. Here, however, we have a sure thing, using that ever-popular magical device— the confederate. Lloyd seems guileless, so he's the perfect choice. Ahead of time, ask him to help you out, and explain what he is to do.

In performance, ask for two volunteers. Choose Dinah, who is fairly cynical, and, of course, Lloyd. Hand each of them a coin, explaining, "I'll turn my back. Then I'd like you to confer. Decide in which hand you'll each hold your coin. When I turn back, both of you should be holding out your fists. I'll try to determine which hands hold the coins." Demonstrate how the coins are to be held by extending your fists palm down.

When you turn back, you examine all four fists, apparently seeking a clue. You'll find a clue when you look at Lloyd's fists. He will have a knuckle slightly extended on the hand in which he holds his coin (Illus. 1). And he will make it a point to have his coin in the hand opposite to that in which Dinah is holding her coin. So, if Lloyd is holding the coin in his left hand, Dinah has hers in the right hand.

Illus. 1

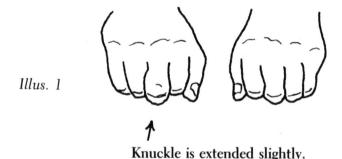

↑
Knuckle is extended slightly.

After some contemplation, you touch Dinah's hand, indicating that this is the one containing the coin. Then you do the same with Lloyd's hand. You can repeat the trick.

Note: If you and your confederate have time to prepare, you might try this for a second repeat. Lloyd asks Dinah which hand he should hold his coin in. Thus, Dinah chooses both for Lloyd and herself. As in the simpler version, Lloyd signals where he is holding the coin by extending a knuckle on the appropriate hand. But, with that same knuckle, he signals the hand in which Dinah is holding her coin. If Dinah is holding the coin in her left hand, he extends the knuckle of his first finger. If she is holding the coin in her right hand, he extends the knuckle of his second finger.

The Power of Three

You will need at least 25 small objects; coins or poker chips are perfect. I usually use coins; they need not all be of the same denomination.

Ask Lucy to assist you in an attempt at telepathy. Place the coins on the table and say to her, "Lucy, I'd like to demonstrate the power of three. For whatever reason, the number three always seems to have mysterious powers. So we'll see if it helps us in this attempt at telepathy."

Turn away and give these directions, with appropriate pauses: "Since three is our magic number, please take a number of the coins and make three equal piles. For example, you might place eight coins in each of three piles. And make sure you have at least four coins in each pile. Arrange the piles in front of you so that you have one on your left, one in the middle, and one on the right.

"The pile on your left is pile 1, the pile in the middle is pile 2, and the pile on your right is pile 3. Again, let's use the power of three. Take *three* coins from pile 1 and place them in pile 2. Now take three coins from pile 3 and place them in pile 2.

"Take the rest of pile 1 away and set these coins aside. Once again, we'll use the power of three. Count the coins in pile 3. Take that number away from pile 2. Discard these.

"I think that the power of three has done its work, so take the rest of the coins from pile 3 and set them aside."

At this point, there are precisely nine coins in pile 2. Ask Lucy to count the remaining coins. "Now please concentrate on that number, Lucy." Eventually, you both concentrate enough so that you are able to tell her that nine is the number she's thinking of.

Here are the steps:
(1) Make three equal piles—1, 2, and 3.
(2) Take three coins from pile 1 and place them on pile 2.
(3) Take three coins from pile 3 and place them in pile 2.
(4) Set aside the rest of pile 1.

(5) Count the coins in pile 3. Take that number from pile 2.

(6) Set aside the rest of pile 3.

(7) There are nine coins in pile 2.

Incidentally, you can repeat the trick, ending up with a different number. Suppose you want to end up with the number five. To get to five, you must take four coins from the nine you would ordinarily end up with (9 − 4 = 5). You do this by inserting this instruction after step 4: "Take four coins from pile 2 and set them aside." Then continue with step 5 to the end.

Notes

If coins or poker chips are not available, the stunt can be performed with any small objects—candies, for instance. Many magicians prefer to perform the trick with playing cards.

Here is one version with playing cards. Hand someone the deck. Then turn your back and give these instructions, with suitable pauses:

"Shuffle the cards, please. Now deal three equal piles in front of you. The number doesn't matter, but all the piles must have the same number of cards in them. And you should have at least five cards in each pile.

"I have no way of knowing how many cards you have chosen to put into each pile. Still, I am going to try to control the number which you will end up with in the middle pile. Would you please choose a number from 1 to 12. This will be the number we should end up with in the middle pile."

The spectator chooses a number. You then continue the instructions.

"You should have three equal piles of cards in a row, right? Take three cards from the pile on the left and place them on the middle pile. Next, take three cards from the pile on the right and place them on the middle pile.

"Count the cards in the pile on the left. Remove this number of cards from the middle pile and place them in the pile on the right."

There are now nine cards in the middle pile. In your next instructions, you manipulate the cards so that the middle pile contains the number of cards chosen by the spectator. For instance, the spectator may have chosen the number seven. Instead of saying, "Remove two cards from the middle pile," you want to create confusion. You might say, "Take one card from the pile on the left and place it in the middle pile. Take three cards from the pile on the right and place them in the middle pile." You've just added four cards to the middle pile, bringing its number to 13. "Take four cards from the middle pile and place them in the pile on the left. Take two cards from the middle pile and place them in the pile on the right." You have just removed six cards from the middle pile, bringing its number to seven.

"I think that should do it. Please count the cards in the middle pile."

Sure enough, you've brought the middle pile to a number selected by a spectator. The trick can be repeated.

It's All in the Hands

In this trick, you must have precisely 20 poker chips or coins on the table. Let's say you're using coins.

Say to Martha, "I'd like you to help me with an experiment in telepathy, using these coins. I'll turn my back and give you some instructions. If you follow them exactly, and if our minds are attuned, I may be able to read your thoughts."

Turn away and give Martha these instructions, with appropriate pauses: "Martha, please pick up a small number of coins in your *right* hand—say, any number up to ten.

"Count the rest of the coins. You have a two-digit number, right? Fine. Add those two digits together. Do you have the number? Good.

"Now take that many *more* coins from the pile on the table and keep those also in your right hand. For instance, suppose you counted 16 coins on the table. You would add the six and one

together, giving you seven. You would pick up seven more coins
from the pile and put them with those in your right hand.

"The last step, Martha. Pick up as many coins as you want in
your left hand. Keep the coins hidden in your hands, Martha,
because I'm going to turn around."

Turn back to Martha and stare deep into her eyes, saying,
"Please concentrate on the coins in your left hand." Brow fur-
rowed, stare into the distance. Look here and there, as you try to
get Martha's thoughts. Casually glance at the coins on the table.
Once more stare into the distance. At last, you tell Martha the
exact number of coins she is holding in her left hand.

How did you do it? Why, you sly rogue, when you glanced at
the coins on the table, you *counted* them. Then you subtracted
the total from nine. This gave you the number of coins held in
Martha's left hand. For instance, you counted five coins on the
table. You subtracted five from nine, giving you four. Martha is
holding four coins in her left hand.

The trick can be repeated, this time with a convincing addition. Have all the coins returned to the table. "That worked
wonderfully, Martha. Let's try it again to make sure it wasn't
coincidence."

Turn your back and give precisely the same directions as before. When you turn back, say, "Now, Martha, which hand shall
we use, your right or your left?"

If she chooses the left hand, go through the same procedure as
before. If she chooses the right hand, you need not concentrate
quite so much; the answer will *always* be eleven.

CARDS

The Date of Your Life

Beforehand, you should know the year in which your subject was born. Find four cards to match the year. For instance, you are going to use Cynthia as your subject. She was born in 1976. Take from the deck an ace, a nine, a seven, and a six. These cards are placed on top of the deck so that the ace is the top card, the nine is second from the top, the seven is third, and the six is fourth. You're ready to perform.

"Cynthia, I wonder if you'll help out. If you do, I'm personally going to see that you get the date of your life. I mean it—the date of your life." This reemphasis is important to the climax of the trick.

Set the deck on the table. "Cynthia, please cut off about half the deck. Place these cards right here." Point to a spot to *your left* of the other pile.

Point to the pile containing your stack. "Cut off half of these and set them here." Point to a spot to your left of the other two piles.

Point to the pile on your right. "And . . . cut off half of these and put them here." Point to a spot to your right of the other three piles.

Point to the pile Cynthia just placed down (the one on your far right). Say, with appropriate pauses, "Please pick this pile up and deal three cards from the top into that spot where the pile rested. Next, deal one card from the top of that packet onto each one of the other three piles." Indicate that she is to deal from *her* left to right. "Now place the packet back in its place." Indicate that she is to replace the packet in the spot on your far right, the place where she dealt off three cards.

Point to the second pile from your right. Have her follow the same procedure with this pile: She deals three cards from the top into the vacated space. Then, going from *her* left to right, she deals one card from the top onto each of the other three piles; she replaces the pile in its original space. Naturally, you guide her through this procedure to make sure no mistakes are made.

You indicate the third pile from your right and have her repeat the dealing routine. Finally, have her do the same with the pile on your far left.

Say to Cynthia, "I'm afraid I have a very personal question to ask. I hope you'll answer it so that we can find out if there is a mystic connection between you and the cards." Pause. "What year were you born in?"

She answers, "Nineteen-seventy-six." At least, you *hope* that's what she answers.

Starting at your right, turn the top card of each pile face up and leave it on its pile. "I promised you the date of your life." Point to each card in turn. "Here we have one, nine, seven, six—1976. If that isn't the date of your life, I don't know what is."

Note: Clearly, you need not use the year of birth for this stunt. Any significant year will do—the year of a promotion, graduation, anniversary, whatever.

Four Among Many

This trick, developed by Roy Walton, uses a principle similar to one I developed in my 1948 booklet, *The Invisible Deck*.

Fan through the deck, faces of the cards towards yourself. Remove four black cards one at a time, placing them in a face-down pile on the table. Continue through the deck, placing *red cards* on the pile. You should put *at least* 20 red cards on the pile. Set the rest of the deck on the table, slightly to your right. This is quite important, as you will see. To the left of the deck is a pile of face-down cards; on the bottom are four black cards, and above them are at least 20 red cards.

As you are doing the preceding, explain, "Every once in a while, if all goes well, an extraordinary coincidence occurs. When this happens, I have no explanation whatever. For this to work, however, I'll need four very sympathetic assistants." Get four spectators to assist you.

Pick up the pile of cards. You will distribute all the cards in the pile to the four spectators. Fan off a group of cards—six or so—from the top and hand them face down to Spectator 1. Say, "Please keep the cards face down." Fan off a similar number of cards and hand them face down to Spectator 2.

As you fan through the cards to decide on how many to give to Spectator 3, reserve exactly *four cards* to give to Spectator 4. Give Spectator 3 his group of cards, and hand the remaining four to Spectator 4. Spectator 4 now holds four black cards; the other spectators, of course, have red cards.

"Without looking at the faces, please mix your cards. Choose one card and give it to me." As each spectator hands you a chosen card, place it in a face-down pile on the table. Spectator 4's card should be on top of the four-card pile.

Take the rest of the cards from the spectators, taking Spectator 4's pile last so that it goes on top. Spread the packet from hand to hand. "You could have chosen any four cards from these." Pick up the four-card pile with your right hand and place it on top, holding a left little-finger break beneath it (Illus. 2). "Instead, you chose these four. Let's take a look at them."

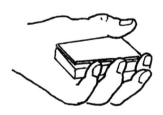

Illus. 2

Illus. 3

You should be holding the packet a few inches above and slightly to the left of the remainder of the deck (Illus. 3). Turn over the top card. "A black card." Even the card on top of the packet. With fingers at the outer edge and thumb at the inner edge, lift off all four cards and set them on top of the deck (Illus. 4). Presumably, you have just placed the top card on top of the deck. The illusion is perfect, Turn over the next card, saying,

Illus. 4

"Another black card." *In exactly the same way as you grasped the packet of four cards,* take this card. Set it on top of the first card, but a bit to the right, so that both can be seen. Do the same with the next two cards. The cards should be sitting on top of the deck as in Illus. 5.

Illus. 5

"What a coincidence! You each chose a black card!" Noting that their reaction is less than enthusiastic, turn over the remaining cards in your hand and quickly fan through them. "And all the rest of these are red!"

Piles of Magic

A number of tricks have been developed using a principle I discovered many years ago and used for several tricks in another booklet called *The Visible Deck.* Here the principle is used in a prediction trick.

Several spectators may assist. I usually use two or three. Let's assume you have three volunteers. Have one of them shuffle the deck and hand it back to you. Fan through the cards, faces towards yourself, saying, "I am going to choose a prediction card." Note the fourth card from the original top of the deck. Fan through the deck again and find the mate to this card—the one that matches it in color and value. This is your prediction card. Remove it from the deck and place it face down onto the table.

"This experiment is dependent on the power of the number nine, which is considered by many to be a mystical number. Nine is also the number of digits in our number system. So we will use nine cards, one to represent each one of the digits."

Count aloud as you deal nine cards into a face-down pile. The card you peeked at is now the 6th card down in this pile. Place the remainder of the deck in front of Spectator 1 and ask him to cut off a pile. Spectator 2 is asked to do the same. Spectator 3 picks up the remainder of the deck.

"I would like you all to count your cards, and then reduce the total to a single digit. For instance, if you count 23 cards, you would have a 2 and a 3. Add the 2 and 3 together, getting 5. If you count 29 cards, you would have a 2 and a 9. Add the 2 and 9 together, getting 11. But, of course, 11 would not be a single digit, so you add the 1 and 1 together, getting 2. Then we'll put all your results together, and reduce *that* total to a single digit. What could be fairer?"

After they count their cards, make sure the spectators understand how to reduce the total to a single digit. Choose a spectator to add the three single digits and then reduce *that* total to a single digit. The result, as I will explain later, is always 6.

Ask one of the spectators to pick up the nine-card pile. "The number that you three freely arrived at was 6, so please deal off six cards." After he deals, have him turn over the last card dealt—the sixth card. "Let's see how my prediction worked out." Turn over your prediction card. The two cards match, of course.

In at least one respect, this trick is quite rare: You *must* do it again! If you don't, spectators might suspect that you always end up with the same number. And, naturally, a repeat with a different number has a powerful impact.

You begin the repeat by taking the two matching cards and setting them aside. No need to comment; just *do it!* Gather up the rest of the cards and have a spectator shuffle them. As before, fan through the deck; this time you note the 6th card from the top. Fan through again, take out the mate to this card, and place this mate face down onto the table. Deal nine cards face down into a pile. The card you peeked at is now 4th from the top.

Proceed exactly as described above. This time, when the totals are reduced to a single digit, the result is 4. The card at the 4th position from the top of the pile matches your prediction card.

Note: Using the basic idea of this trick, you may decide to devise a trick of your own. Here is an explanation of the principle I discovered so long ago: With a 52-card deck, you will always end up with the digit 7. Prove it to yourself. Divide the deck into as many piles as you wish. Count all the piles. Reduce each pile to a single digit by continuing to add the numbers together until you get a single digit. In the same way, reduce the totals to a single digit. No matter how you do it, the single digit will be 7. Why? Because you had 52 cards—and $5 + 2 = 7$. In the same way, if you had 51 cards, the final digit would always be 6 $(5 + 1)$.

To demonstrate, let's divide up that 52-card deck. You have one pile of 11 cards, one of 24 cards, and one of 17 cards—a total of 52. Let's reduce each pile.

$$11 \text{ cards} \quad 1 + 1 = 2$$

$$24 \text{ cards} \quad 2 + 4 = 6$$

$$17 \text{ cards} \quad 1 + 7 = 8$$

The respective totals are 2, 6, and 8. Add them up, and you get 16. Add 1 and 6, and you get—that's right!—7.

The first time you perform the trick I just described, you have set one card aside as your prediction. You have dealt nine other cards onto the table. Therefore, the spectators divide up a 42-card packet and end up with the digit 6.

On the repeat, you also set aside a card as your prediction, but you also set aside the two cards that matched. Again you dealt nine other cards onto the table. 1 + 2 + 9 = 12. You take 12 cards from 52, and you get 40. So the spectators divide up a 40-card packet, and will always end up with the digit 4.

Double Mental Miracle

F. J. Baker, using a clever old principle, developed a mental trick which has everything: audience participation, mystery, and a seemingly impossible conclusion. I have revised his method of setting up the cards at the beginning to make it faster and—I believe—slightly more logical. As the trick stood, there was a slim possibility of failure at the end. I have added a wrinkle which ensures success.

Have the deck shuffled and returned to you. You are now going to set up about half the deck so that the cards alternate red–black. "We are going to attempt an extremely difficult experiment in telepathy. For this, we will need exactly the right cards—cards that are easy to remember." Starting at the bottom, fan through the cards, faces toward yourself. Stop at the first red card that is followed by a black card. Perhaps you will be lucky enough to find that another red card and black card follow this. If so, pull these four from the deck and set them face down in a pile on the table. Find another group of red-black cards; let's say that this group consists of red-black-red-black-red-black. You would pull these from the deck and place them face down on top of the others. You are gradually building a pile of cards on the table in which the bottom card is red and the cards alternate red and black throughout.

As you do this, comment: "Yes, we need very special cards. Ah, these will do very well." Continue fanning. "No, no. Ah, here's another good bunch." As you add to the pile, you must, of course, remember the color of the last card you placed on the pile. So, as the cards go onto the pile, you think to yourself,

"Red, black, red, black, red, black, etc."

You can fan back and forth through the deck since the removal of groups often causes other red-black groups to develop. When you have about half the deck arranged in a face-down pile on the table, stop and set the rest of the deck aside. "This should be enough."

Since the bottom card of the tabled packet is red, it is vital that the last card you place on the packet be black.

You continue: "Now I need two volunteers." From the many eager spectators who hold up their hands, screaming, "Me, me!" you choose Marilyn and Avery.

Meanwhile, pick up your stacked group and hold them in the overhand shuffle position. Casually pick up the bottom portion with your right hand and drop it on top. Repeat this procedure. Done casually and rapidly, you seem to be giving the cards an overhand shuffle. Actually, you are simply performing complete cuts, which do not affect your red–black order.

Have Marilyn and Avery approach the table. Set the stacked group on the table, saying, "Marilyn, I'd like you to give the cards a complete cut." When she finishes, have Avery also give the cards a complete cut. Then have Marilyn cut the cards once more. "Three times is the charm," you explain. "Now no one here has any way of knowing what the top two cards of that packet are, right? So, Marilyn, give that top card to Avery. And you take the next card yourself. Each of you look at your card and commit it to memory. But don't let anyone else see the card." When they are done, continue: "Now, Avery, please put your card back on top of the packet." He does so. "And Marilyn, please put your card back on top."

At this point, the entire packet is in proper red–black order, *except* for the top two cards. Once more, go through the procedure of having the packet cut three times.

"We're going to try to perform two miracles, so we'll need two packets of cards. Marilyn, will you please deal the cards into two packets." Make sure that she deals the cards alternately—first one to the left, then one to the right, and so on.

"Hand me one of the packets, please." You take the cards and fan through them. "Will you both think of the card you chose." You will notice that all of the cards you hold are of one color, except for one card. Let's say all the cards are black, except for the nine of hearts. Remove this from the packet and hold it up, saying, "Which one of you chose the nine of hearts?" Marilyn admits that it's her card.

"So I have discovered your card telepathically. But then I'm *supposed* to be able to do that. Let's try for a *real* miracle."

For this next portion of the trick, you must pick out someone who is quite bright *and* a good sport. "Larry, would you mind helping out." He agrees to assist. "Avery, please give Larry that other packet of cards."

Larry takes the packet. "Now step aside from the rest of the group, Larry, so that you can concentrate better." Actually, you don't want anyone else to see the faces of the cards when Larry fans the packet out.

"Avery, I'd like you to concentrate on your card. Larry, please fan the cards out so that you can see the faces. Look at each and every card. As you do so, one card should stand out in your mind above all the rest."

Pause. While speaking to Larry, you have added the packet in your hand to the deck and nonchalantly given the deck a shuffle. And then you have set the deck on the table.

"Larry, does one card stand out?" He says yes. "Take that card from the packet and hold it up so that no one else can see its face."

Chances are overwhelming that Larry has removed the one black card from the packet of red cards. But you're going to provide yourself with a little insurance policy. Take the rest of the packet from Larry and fan through the packet, faces towards yourself. "So you had strong feelings about *one* card from this rather large packet of cards, right?" You are only incidentally building suspense; you want to make sure he's holding the right card. If he's not, cut the right card to the top of the packet. Drop the packet on top of the deck.

"What card did you choose, Avery?" He names it. Have Larry turn his card around so that all can see it. A telepathic miracle! Suppose, however, you know that Larry has the wrong card. As above, you ask Avery to name his card. Ask Larry to turn his card around. As he does so, casually pick up the top card of the deck. "Oh-oh! Wrong card, Larry." Hold up the card you're holding. "I think this one would be a bit more like it."

As far as anyone else knows, this is the way the trick is supposed to end. In either instance, give the deck a casual shuffle, eliminating the evidence.

To close, say to Larry, "Don't worry about it, Larry. After all, I *am* a professional."

Mind Control

Some time ago I developed a trick based on a little-known "mathematical" principle. I was never quite satisfied with the climax to the trick, however. So, after considerable experimentation, I developed this version. It's simple, direct, and surprising, and it has considerable audience participation.

Ask Gene to remove seven black cards and seven red cards from the deck. You explain that seven is a mystical number. (Actually, any number will work.) Have him shuffle the packet and return it to you. Say, "In a moment, I am going to ask you to select any seven cards you wish. *But*, if all goes well, your selections will actually be controlled by my mind. Apparently you will be making free choices, but you will actually be under my control." Stare at Gene for a moment; then nod your head. "Yes, I think so. This should work."

Pause; then continue: "Have you ever played odds and evens with someone? Each of you flips a coin. One of you calls odds or evens. If both coins land on the same side, that's evens, and the person who has evens wins. If the coins have opposite sides, the person who has odds wins. To see if my attempt at mind control works, we'll play odds and evens with these cards. We'll use the reds and the blacks. If both cards are red or both cards are black, that's evens. If one is black and one is red, that's odds. Now I'll arrange the cards so that you'll take the ones I want you to."

Fan through the cards that Gene removed from the deck, with the faces towards yourself. Move cards around until the blacks and reds are separated. All the blacks should be on top, and all the reds on the bottom, or vice versa. Turn the packet face down and hold it in your left hand. With your left thumb, push off the top card and take it with your palm-up right hand. "Gene, you're going to choose seven cards. Do you want this one?" If he says yes, have him take the card and place it face down in front of him. If he doesn't, offer the next card, holding it *beneath* the first card.

You continue offering individual cards in the same way. Gene places his selections into a pile in front of him; you take the rejects *one under the other* in your right hand.

Count Gene's selections aloud, reminding him from time to time that he must choose seven cards. When he has chosen his seventh card, take the remainder (if any) beneath the ones you're holding in your right hand. Set your cards on the table. "You have a stack, and I have a stack. You had complete freedom of choice in selecting your cards—*unless* I was able to mentally control your selections."

Now you engage in a bit of ambiguity. "Now we'll play odds or evens. If the two cards are the same color, it's evens. If the two cards are different colors, it's odds. I'd like you to choose one of them for me—odds or evens."

If the spectator says odds, you say, "Okay, you chose odds for me. And you have evens." If he says evens, you say, "Okay, you chose evens. That leaves me with odds."

(The ambiguity is in the expression "I'd like you to choose one of them for me—odds or evens." The "for me" can either mean, "Choose odds or evens, and it will be for me," or it could mean, "Do me the favor of choosing either odds or evens for yourself.")

Each of you turns over the top card of his pile and places it in the middle. The colors will not match. "Odds," you say. "One for me." You pick up the two cards, turn them face down, and place them in a pile near you.

Again you turn over your top cards. Once more you win. "Ah, another one. So far, so good." Turn these two face down and put them on the pile where you placed the others.

Continue through the rest. You win every turn, of course. "Thanks so much, Gene. I couldn't have done it without you."

DICE

Feel Your Way

There is an old parlor trick in which a magician claims he can tell the number on top of a die which is placed in his hand behind his back. Facing the audience with the die behind his back, the magician presses the third finger of his right hand firmly against the top of the die, thus getting an imprint on his finger. Holding the die in his other hand, he then brings the right hand forward and, in wiping his brow, looks at the imprint and sees what the number is.

The stunt is not only cumbersome, but also frequently fails. I, for example, seldom could get a good impression on my finger. And it does not enhance the trick if you stand there, peering intently at your finger, trying to decipher the number of dots.

I worked out an easy method to accomplish the same trick. Announce, "Some people have a real affinity for dice. In fact, I know of some people who seem to have ·the ability to win in almost any game in which dice are involved. Call it luck; call it what you will. In a small way, I have a similar ability. If someone places a die in my hand behind my back, I can usually tell you what the top number is."

It is best if you either borrow the die or have someone choose one from several you've provided. Turn your back to the group. Have someone note the top number of a die and then place the die on your outstetched right hand. Slowly turn until you are facing the group.

Carefully pick the die up between your left thumb and first finger. Your right thumb and first finger take an identical grip, thumb below and first finger on top (Illus. 6). Using your *right first finger,* you now count the number of spots on the top of the die.

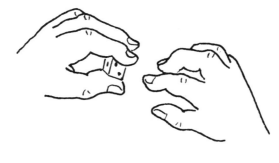

Illus. 6

First move the tip of your finger along the top right side as you count the number of depressions. I find it best to sort of drag the fingernail across the surface, along with a portion of the skin at the tip of the finger. Next you move your finger across the top center of the die, and then across the top left side. If you're not sure, start again at the top right side.

With a bit of practice, you can discover the number quite rapidly. And, of course, you can repeat the stunt as often as you wish.

Stacked Dice

I recently came up with a slight variation of a trick by Frank Dodd.

You will need three dice and a willing spectator. Stella would be a good choice. Toss the three dice onto the table, saying to Stella, "Would you please examine the dice. Roll them several times so that you can see that they are ordinary in every way."

When she finishes, say, "Stella, I would like you to concentrate on a number, and then see if I can divine that number. I'm pretty good at it. Quite often, I get the exact number. But, of course, sometimes I fail. It all depends on whether our minds connect.

"But, to make sure you won't be making any sort of psychological choice, you must choose a number by chance. So, when I turn my back, here's what I'd like you to do: Roll out the dice and then stack them one on top of the other in any way you wish." Demonstrate by rolling out the dice and then stacking them *evenly* one on top of the other (Illus. 7). Hand Stella the dice. Turn away, saying, "Tell me when you're done."

Illus. 7

When Stella says she is ready, turn back briefly saying, "Please cup one of your hands around the dice so that no one else can see the numbers. I don't want you to think that anyone is helping me." You have already turned away again as you complete your comments. *But* you have noticed the number which is on the top of the uppermost die. Let's assume that the number you noted was six.

Continue your instructions, with appropriate pauses: "You have three dice, one sitting on top of the other. The top die and the one below it have numbers that are touching. These would be the *bottom* number of the die on top and the *top* number of the middle die. Please lift off the top die, look at the touching numbers, and add them together. Remember this total. Now toss the top die to one side, making sure it rolls over several times.

"Two dice are now sitting one on top of the other. The top die and the bottom die have two numbers that are touching. Please look at these two numbers and add them together. Now add that total to your previous total, and please remember the result.

Again, toss the top die to one side, making sure it rolls over several times.

"Only one die remains on the table. Turn that over and look at the number on the bottom. Add that to your total. This total is your final number, which I would like you to concentrate on. Please roll that last die to one side so that there'll be no evidence of what that last number was."

Turn and face the group. "Stella, we made sure that you selected a number completely by chance. Please visualize that number, while I try to connect with your mind." Gradually, you reveal a number, and Stella admits that you are correct.

There's really nothing to it. Early on, you noted the number on top of the stack of dice. Simply subtract this from 21, and you have the final result. In our example, the top die showed a 6. You subtract 6 from 21, getting 15. The final number Stella comes up with will be 15.

Review

(1) A spectator stacks three dice.

(2) You note the top number on the top die and mentally subtract it from 21 to get the number you will name later.

(3) The spectator lifts off the top die and adds the two surfaces that were touching. She rolls the top die to one side.

(4) She lifts off the next die and adds the two touching surfaces. She adds the result to her total and then rolls the die she is holding to one side.

(5) She looks at the number on the bottom of the last die and adds this to her total. She rolls this last die to one side.

(6) You name the total, and the spectator verifies it.

Notes
The trick is based on a fairly well known principle: The opposite sides of any die always add up to 7. But here the principle is extremely well disguised.

Occasionally a spectator will get the math wrong. When you name a number and she says that you're wrong, simply say, "As I pointed out, I don't always get the right number. Let's try another experiment." After all, you have conducted an experiment in telepathy, and no psychic—not even your magnificent self—is 100 percent perfect every time.

Simple Addition

For your next demonstration of mind reading, you will need three dice. You will also need the assistance of a spectator. Let's say that Gus agrees to help.

"Gus, I would like you to roll the three dice several times to make sure they are ordinary in every way."

Turn your back. "Now, Gus, I'd like you to roll out the three dice and add up the top numbers. Do you have your total? Please remember that number. Now pick up any *one* of the dice, turn it over, and look at the bottom number. Add that to your total." Pause. "Please roll out that same die. Whatever number comes up, add that to your total."

When he is done, turn back. "Gus, there is no way I could possibly know which die you selected to roll twice. So, there is no way I could know the number you arrived at. Please put that total at the forefront of your mind. *Think* of it. I'll try to get the number."

As you focus your brain on Gus's thoughts, you focus even more on the dice on the table. Total the values and add seven. This gives you Gus's number.

How does this work? The two sides of a die always add up to seven. Gus has tossed out three dice and picked up one of them. He knows the total on the other two dice, and so will you when you turn around. Gus has already added in one side of the die; now he adds in the other side. So the die he has picked up will always produce seven. Thus far, his number is the total of the two dice on the table plus seven. He rolls out the die he is holding.

The number shown is added to his total. So, his number is the total of the two numbers left on the table, plus the number on the die he has just rolled, plus seven.

Notes

(1) The principle is so cleverly concealed that you will even fool those who *know* that the two sides of a die total seven.

(2) The trick may be repeated . . . *once*.

(3) To make sure no mistakes are made in the addition, you might appoint two assistants.

The Power of Seven

You will need two dice, a deck of cards, and a cooperative spectator. Lenore is always eager to help; why not give her a chance?

Hand Lenore the deck, saying, "Please give the deck a good shuffle." When she finishes, say, "We are going to use two dice and some playing cards. With dice, as you know, seven is a very special number. And it is also considered a good-luck number. Now we will try to establish a relationship between the cards and the dice. So please deal out seven cards into a pile, and set the rest of the deck aside."

Turn away. "Now, Lenore, please roll out the dice. You can roll them any number of times. When you have two numbers that you're satisfied with, stop rolling." When she is ready, continue, with appropriate pauses: "Now note the number on top of one of the dice. Pick up that die and hide it. You can put it in your pocket or let somebody else hold it concealed in his hand. Next pick up the seven cards. Count down to the number you noted on the die and look at the card that lies at that number in the pile. Remember the name of that card and leave it at that number in the pile. In other words, if the number you noted on the die was four, you would look at the fourth card down in the pile of seven cards. You would remember that card and leave it at that fourth position."

When Lenore is finished, turn back. Pick up the packet, saying, "I have no way of knowing where your selected card is in this packet. Certainly the die on the table won't help me. Still, I'm going to mix the cards and see if fate, along with the power of seven, will help me find your card."

Place the packet behind your back. Note the number showing on the die on the table. Add one to this number. For example, if the die is showing four, add one to get the number five. Move this number of cards, one at a time, from the bottom to the top of the packet. Bring the packet forward and hand it to Lenore.

"Lenore, I would like you to bring out the hidden die and place it on the table so that its original number is on top." She does so. "I did not know this number, but—as I indicated before—the number seven may have established an affinity between the cards and the dice. Add the numbers on the two dice. Now move one card from the top to the bottom for each number in the total." Suppose the total is nine. "You can see that the total is nine. One at a time, move nine cards from the top to the bottom."

When she finishes, say, "What was the card you looked at, Lenore?" She names it. "Please turn over the top card." It's the chosen card. By golly, there *was* an affinity between the cards and the dice.

SIGNALS

These seven mental effects always require two persons—one to signal, the other to receive the signal. In the first two of these, your assistant is actually a confederate.

In the others, you will be assisted by a medium—someone who is ostensibly very sensitive to telepathic messages. Choose your medium carefully. You want someone who can play-act, who will strain as she strives to receive the mental waves. Particularly, you want someone who won't laugh out loud.

Count on the Fingers of One Hand

"I am going to test my clairvoyance," you announce. "For this I will need the services of three volunteers." You are delighted when Dan, Linda, and Christine all volunteer.

"When I turn my back, I would like two of you to hold up a number of fingers on one hand. We'll use Dan and Linda for this. And Christine, you'll be the announcer. When they hold up their fingers, you announce the total. Then I'll try to figure out the exact number of fingers that each person is holding up."

In this example, you turn away, and Christine announces a total of seven. You instantly say, "Dan is holding up four fingers, and Linda is holding up three." Correct!

Again the two hold up fingers. Christine tells you the total is five. You say, "Dan is holding up one finger, and Linda is holding up four."

You can continue on ad infinitum. At the group's insistence, you may change announcers; after all, Christine might be giving you secret signals. You may also replace Dan, in case they think he may be doing something sneaky. But when it comes time to replace Linda, quit. Because she is your confederate.

She starts out by holding up three fingers. You hear that the total is seven, so you know that Dan must be holding up four fingers. Next, Linda will hold up the number of fingers that Dan was holding up the previous time. So she holds up four fingers. The total is five, so you know that Dan is holding up one finger, and Linda is holding up four. Next time, she will hold up one finger.

If Dan is replaced, Linda will start by holding up three fingers again.

This is the sneakiest and easiest use of a confederate that I know of.

Getting a Handle

Once more you will use a confederate. (In magic biz, we often refer to such a person as a stooge; but when talking to the stooge, we use the word *confederate*. To complete your education in the nomenclature of stoogeology, a *plant* is also a stooge or confederate, and is usually quite cooperative, but not responsible for the success of the trick.)

You confer with Melissa, your confederate, ahead of time. The only prop you'll need is an ordinary cup which you place on a table.

In performance, you announce, "I have discovered, ladies and gentlemen, that I have the mystic gift of telling time." Pause. "Thank you so much. Yes, I can look at a watch and tell you the right time within—oh—30 minutes. That's with my watch." Address one of the spectators: "Let's see how I do with *your* watch. In a moment I'll leave the room. When I'm gone, I'd like you to set your watch for some exact hour—two o'clock, three o'clock, four o'clock, whatever. Then place your watch on the table."

Look around the room. "I'll need a volunteer, someone who's very tidy. Ah, Melissa. Would you mind helping out." If she does mind, you'd better start another trick. "After the watch is placed on the table, Melissa, I'd like you to cover it with the cup. So just turn the cup over, cover the watch, and make sure that no part of the watch sticks out. Okay?"

You leave the room. When called back, you glance at the cup, and then look the owner of the watch right in the eye and tell him what time he has on his watch. For instance, "Nine o'clock!" Melissa turns the cup over and looks at the watch. "Why, it *is* nine o'clock!"

But, of course, Melissa had already noted the time on the watch. And, when she covered the watch, she made sure the cup handle pointed to the proper hour (Illus. 8). It's easy enough for her to get the handle just right as she makes sure the watch is tucked under the cup properly.

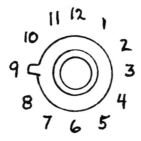

The cup viewed from above.

Illus. 8

Melissa and you have agreed ahead of time on how the cup will be oriented. Twelve o'clock will be at the far end of the table, for instance. Or, if you think it necessary to be devious, the "clock" will be upside down as you look at it.

If you feel brave, you might repeat the stunt with another spectator.

Just a Case of Cards

In the next five tricks, Frieda will be the mentalist. And you will be the one trying to communicate with her telepathically.

I have devised an improved signalling method for this old trick.

Start things rolling by saying, "Ladies and gentlemen, it is my great pleasure at this time to introduce one of the great mind readers of our time. A round of applause, please, for that magnificent mistress of mentalism, the Fabulous Frieda!" After taking a bow, Frieda leaves the room.

You remove the cards from a card case and hand them to a spectator, saying, "Please shuffle the cards." When he is finished, continue: "Now deal five cards face up onto the table. Just spread them around; they need not be in any particular order." After the five cards are dealt out, say, "Set the rest of the deck down anywhere."

Ask another spectator to touch any one of the cards. After the card is touched, you set the card case onto the table. Ask one of the spectators to call Frieda back. When she returns, she walks directly to the table and studies the cards. Eventually, she touches the chosen one.

Obviously, you signal the card, but how? You use the card case. But first you must assign each card on the table a number from 1 to 5. The lowest value will be number 1, the next higher card will be number 2, and so on, with the highest card being number 5. When two cards of the same value are among those on the table, you will distinguish them by suit, using the well-known clubs-hearts-spades-diamonds order (CHaSeD). Clubs would be the lowest value and diamonds the highest.

Let's try an example. Suppose these cards are tossed face up onto the table: 9C, 7H, JS, 7D, 3C. The 3C is the lowest value, so it is number 1. The next higher values are the two sevens. The 7H is assigned number 2, because hearts comes before diamonds in the CHaSeD order. The 7D then becomes number 3. 9C is number 4, and JS is number 5.

1 - 3C

2 - 7H

3 - 7D

4 - 9C

5 - JS

You use the card case to signal one of the five numbers. At the beginning you remove the cards from the card case and hand them to a spectator. *Continue holding the card case.* The spectator shuffles the deck, deals out five cards face up, and sets the rest of the deck aside. Another spectator touches a card. "Complete freedom of choice," you declare. "In fact, you can change your mind if you wish." After the card is finally chosen, you know which number you must signal: 1, 2, 3, 4, or 5.

One side of the card case has a little moon cut out of it so that you can get your thumb under the flap. Think of this "moon side" as the *front* of the card case. This will help you remember that this is where you *start* with the numbers. If you wish to signal number 1, you casually toss the card case onto the table, moon side up, with the flap out. For number 2, the card case has the moon side up, but the flap is tucked in.

Numbers 3 and 4 are signalled with the *back* side of the card case up. If the flap is out, the number is 3. If the flap is tucked in, the number is 4.

How do you signal number 5? The card does not go onto the table. Stick it into your pocket or simply toss it somewhere other than on the table.

Ask someone to call Frieda back. She notes the card case (or the absence of it) and converts the number you signalled to the appropriate card.

Needless to say, Frieda should not immediately look at the card case. All her attention should be on the cards. (It will take her a little time to figure out the proper number order anyway.) As she studies the cards, she can casually sneak a peek at the card case. Then, to be on the safe side, she should continue to study the cards for a while before making her selection.

Notes

(1) When you are preparing to make your signal with the card case, you must be very nonchalant. While you are sticking the flap in, for instance, continue chatting. Say things like, "You made a very good choice. I doubt that even the Fabulous Frieda will be able to divine your card. But we'll hope for the best."

(2) If you choose, you may leave the room before Frieda is called back. This can enhance the trick. If you decide to do this, simply take the card case with you when you're signalling the number 5.

(3) You might perform the stunt once more, casually picking up the card case as the spectator reshuffles the deck and deals out five more cards. One repetition is plenty; no use tempting fate.

Body Language

Wayne Van Zandt developed a set of signals in a method he called "Around the Clock." Based on this, I developed a simple method which can be learned in five minutes.

Frieda leaves the room. You spread a deck of cards face up on a table. Invite a spectator to come up and touch one of the cards. When Frieda is called back by a spectator, she looks at you, at the group, at the deck. Gradually—naming color, suit, and then value—she reveals the name of the card. The spectator says that Frieda is right. The experiment is repeated several times.

It doesn't really matter how the spectator touches the card; the important thing is that you know what the card is. Equally important is your position in the room when Frieda returns. You should be facing Frieda when she reenters the room. And you should be standing among the spectators or behind them.

How do you signal Frieda? First, by pretending you're a clock. The hour you indicate is the same as the value of the selected card.

Let's move around the clock:

1 o'clock = Hold your left shoulder with your right hand.

2 o'clock = Grip your left bicep with your right hand.

3 o'clock = Grip your left elbow with your right hand.

4 o'clock = Hold your left forearm with your right hand.

5 o'clock = Hold your left wrist with your right hand.

6 o'clock = Clasp your hands in front of you.

7 o'clock = Hold your right wrist with your left hand.

8 o'clock = Hold your right forearm with your left hand.

9 o'clock = Grip your right elbow with your left hand.

10 o'clock = Grip your right bicep with your left hand.

11 o'clock = Hold your right shoulder with your left hand.

12 o'clock = Place either hand under your chin.

To signal 13, let both arms hang by your side.

When Frieda steps back into the room, all she needs to do to get the value of the chosen card is *to read you like a clock*. (1 is an ace, 11 is a jack, 12 is a queen, and 13 is a king.)

When signalling, it is vital that you strike a nonchalant pose. To signal the number 1, for instance, you don't seize your left shoulder with your right hand. Instead, you assume a relaxed position, perhaps rub the shoulder briefly, or casually scratch it. As soon as you're sure Frieda has noted the hour you are signalling, assume another pose.

The suit? This is signalled in a similar way. The order of clubs-hearts-spades-diamonds (CHaSeD) is again used. And you signal *with your eyes* (Illus. 9). If the suit is clubs, you look to the left. If the suit is hearts, you look down. If the suit is spades, you look to the right. If the suit is diamonds, you look up. To put it another way:

Clubs = Eyes at 3 o'clock

Hearts = Eyes at 6 o'clock

Spades = Eyes at 9 o'clock

Diamonds = Eyes at 12 o'clock

12 o'clock, diamonds

9 o'clock, spades

3 o'clock, clubs

6 o'clock, hearts

Illus. 9

Frieda should not have to stare at you, waiting for the signal with the eyes. When she enters, she immediately catches your signal of the value, and you promptly stop signalling. *Immediately*, signal the suit with your eyes and hold the signal until you're sure she has it.

The Table Tells

There is nothing wrong with an old method of signalling, providing that it is not well known. Such is the case here.

You will require a pen, a sheet of paper, a table, and the ever-psychic Frieda. Naturally, Frieda starts things rolling by leaving the room.

Place the pen and paper on the table and say to a spectator, "I would like you to think of any number from 1 to 99. And then we'll see if Frieda can divine the number. To make it easier to visualize the number, would you please write it down on the paper." Before the spectator writes, add: "If you wish to change your mind and choose a different number, you may do so."

Once the number has been written down, you take the pen, set it on the table, and say, "Now please fold up the paper so that no one else can see the number." (Of course, *you* already have seen the number.)

You take the folded paper and place it on the table. At this point, you may leave the room or stay, as someone calls Frieda back.

When Frieda returns, she divines the number. Before she does so, however, she may examine the pen. She may even pick up the folded paper and hold it to her forehead. It doesn't matter, for Frieda immediately knows the number when she sees where you have placed the pen and paper.

Let's assume that you are working on a rectangular table. When Frieda reenters the room, she should be facing a long side of the table. (If this is impossible, arrange a mutual orientation ahead of time.) As she faces the table, Frieda should picture the top of the table as shown in Illus. 10.

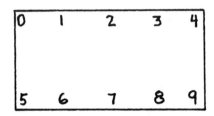

Top view of table
as visualized by Frieda.

Illus. 10

When you take the pen from the spectator, you place it at the position of the first digit of the selected number. When you take the paper, you place it at the second digit of the selected number. Thus, if the chosen number was 35, you would place the pen and paper at the positions shown in Illus. 11.

Top view of table.

Pencil is at 3;
paper is at 5.

Illus. 11

It is quite easy for you or Frieda to figure out the numbers. The exact middle on the far side is the digit 2, and the exact middle on the near side is the digit 7. The end numbers are easy, of course. And the other numbers are halfway between the middle and the end.

If the spectator should choose a single digit number, simply place the pen on the imagined zero and place the paper on the appropriate digit. If both digits are the same, place both objects on the same digit.

Note: Sometimes the only table available is perfectly square, like a card table. The trick will work just as well. Ahead of time, you and Frieda must agree on how she will face the table.

Incidentally, as tempting as the prospect is, this is probably not a good trick to repeat.

The Sky's the Limit

Ben Christopher developed a mental trick involving an extremely subtle method of signalling. I have worked out a variation suitable for any size group. In addition, obscure symbols were involved in the original trick; I have changed them to symbols that are more comprehensible.

Mentalists often use a slate and chalk to demonstrate their ability to predict the future. You may use them for this trick. But I prefer paper and pen. In addition, you will need a magazine. You will also need to prepare four cards. The size doesn't matter, really, but I like to take two 3 × 5 file cards and neatly cut them in half. On one side of each card you will draw one of these figures: crescent moon, sun, star, comet (see Illus. 12 on the next page). Note that the name of each figure is printed below it; as you will see, this is the key to the trick.

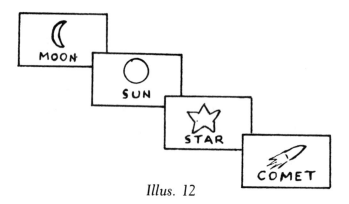

Illus. 12

Once more, Frieda will be the medium. She goes into another room as you explain the procedure to the spectators. "For centuries man has been fascinated by the mysteries of the sky—the planets, the stars, the sun, the moon, and so on. Frequently mystics study these heavenly objects, trying to establish a relationship between them and human conduct and events. We'll use four symbols of these celestial objects in a simple telepathic test." As you continue, hold up the cards one by one. "Here we have the moon, the sun, a star, and a comet. Now I need someone to volunteer as our telepath."

Kate volunteers. "Kate, I don't know whether you have telepathic ability, but Fabulous Frieda certainly does. Perhaps with both of you trying your best, we will have mental communication . . . and success. First, take these cards and mix them any way you wish. When you're done, choose one." After she picks one, say, "Now let's distribute the rest to three other persons. Volunteers?" Make sure that you select three persons who are sitting some distance from Kate.

When this chore is done, hand Kate a sheet of paper and a pen. "Anywhere on that sheet, Kate, draw the symbol you've selected. Please make it as much like the symbol on the card as you can." Give Kate a magazine to place beneath the paper as she draws. After she finishes, take the paper and magazine together, along with the pen, and hand them to one of the other volunteers, saying, "Will you please draw your symbol anywhere on the sheet."

In handing the material to the next volunteer, you make sure that Kate's drawing is now *upside down*. It is most likely that Kate will hand you the drawing so that it is upside down as you look at it. If so, casually turn it end for end as you pass it to the next volunteer. If Kate should hand you the drawing right-side up as you look at it, simply hand it directly to the next volunteer. While taking the material and passing it on, chat a bit to provide misdirection. For instance, you might comment on how Kate must have had years of art training to have done such a magnificent job.

The next two times you pass the material on, you do not reverse the paper and magazine. The result is that Kate's is the only drawing which has been reversed.

Have yet another volunteer take the sheet and magazine, along with the pen, to Frieda. (Actually, anyone but Kate will do.) Explain to the group, "Frieda will try to identify our volunteer telepath. So, I'd like you, Kate, to concentrate on your symbol."

When your volunteer returns with the paper, take it and ask Kate, "What symbol did you select, Kate?" She names it. You hold up the paper, showing that every symbol except hers has been obliterated. "So, Frieda, with Kate's help, has correctly identified the symbol selected by our telepath. Congratulations, Kate."

The minute Frieda saw the paper, she knew which symbol had been chosen. It was the only one on the page which was upside down. If no symbol was upside down, Frieda would know that the sun had been chosen. If you study the symbols in Illus. 13 again, you will note that the crescent *moon* has its ends pointing to the right, the *comet* is pointing to the right, and the *star* is standing on two points. Clearly if the moon or comet is pointing to the left, that is the chosen symbol. And if the star is standing on *one* point, that is the chosen symbol. If none of the three is upside down, then the sun is the chosen symbol.

It is vital that each symbol be drawn exactly as pictured on the card. So the name of each symbol is printed on the bottom to provide proper orientation.

The pen must be a fairly wide-pointed marker type so that when Frieda eliminates the other symbols, she can color them out completely.

Note: If you elect to use a slate and chalk, Frieda simply erases the other symbols.

Murder, She Says

I have combined some subtle principles in this trick, one of my favorite mental effects. The signalling methods are deceptively simple. You will need a fair-size group.

Frieda, as usual, is in another room. "Let's play a game of murder," you suggest. "I need some volunteers." Pick out two women and two men. One of the women should be notably taller than the other, and the same for the two men.

Have the four volunteers stand or, if there is room, move to the front of the group.

"Now you must decide who the murderer will be. And you must also decide on a victim. I will offer no suggestions whatever."

The entire group participates in the process. Finally, a murderer and a victim are chosen from among the four volunteers. Take an object from your pocket, let's say a house key (any object will do). Hand the key to the murderer, saying, "To help Frieda get the proper vibrations, please hold this in your hand for a moment." Also, have the victim hold the key briefly.

Request that one of the other members of the group notify Frieda that she can return. While this is being done, you leave the room. When Frieda returns, she rubs the key, carefully inspects the faces of the four volunteers, concentrates fiercely, and then identifies both the murderer and the victim.

How? To begin with, you pass on to Frieda the sex of the murderer. You do this by having her notified by a member of the opposite sex.

If the murderer is tall, have the messenger go get her. If the murderer is short, have the messenger *call* to Frieda. So, Frieda immediately knows the murderer.

How does Frieda know the victim? You have asked someone else in the group to provide Frieda with the key. (We will call this individual the *key-person*.) The key-person is of the same sex as the victim. If this person hands her the key, the victim is tall. If this person points out the key on the table, the victim is short.

An example: Of the four volunteers, the tall man is the murderer and the short woman is the victim. Since a man is the murderer, a *woman* from the group will be the messenger. Since the murderer is tall, you say to the messenger, "When I leave the room, will you please go get Frieda and ask her to join the group." (If the murderer were short, you would ask the messenger to call to Frieda.)

Frieda now knows that the murderer is a tall man.

The victim is a woman, so the key-person must also be a woman. Since the victim is short, the key-person will indicate that the key is on the table. You tell her, "When Frieda comes in, please tell her that the key is on the table, but please don't touch it yourself." (If the murderer were tall, you would hand the key to the key-person and tell her to give it to Frieda.)

Frieda now knows that the victim is a short woman.

Review

The Murderer

(1) The messenger is of the opposite sex to the murderer.
(2) If the messenger goes to Frieda (makes personal contact),

the murderer is *tall*. If the messenger calls to Frieda, the murderer is *short*.

The Victim

(1) The key-person is of the same sex as the victim.

(2) If the key-person hands Frieda the key (makes personal contact), the victim is *tall*. If the key-person indicates that the key is on the table, the victim is *short*.

NUMBERS

For all of the mental tricks with numbers, paper and a writing instrument should be readily available. In some of these tricks, a calculator may be used instead of paper and pen or pencil. To simplify, I will always assume that you are using a pen.

Predicting on the Square

Martin Gardner developed this simple but effective trick.

Say to the group, "I am going to try to predict an outcome based on complete freedom of choice." Hold up a sheet of paper. "On this side of the sheet of paper, I am putting my prediction." Without letting anyone see, write the number 15 on the paper. Turn the paper over so that the blank side is up. Draw on the paper a 3 × 3 grid, and number the squares from 1 to 9, as shown in Illus. 13.

Illus. 13

If you prefer, you can just put down three tidy rows, without the grid.

Let's say that Joyce volunteers to help out. Say to her, "Joyce, I'd like you to circle any number, and then cross out the other numbers in that same row and column." Suppose she chooses the number 4. The result will be as shown in Illus. 14.

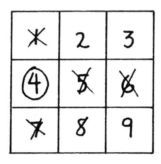

Illus. 14

"Please circle another number, one which hasn't been crossed out. Again, cross out the other numbers in that same row and column." Suppose she chooses the number 9. The result will be as shown in Illus. 15.

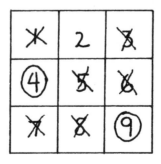

Illus. 15

"Finally, just circle the number which has not been crossed out." After she does so, continue: "Please add up the circled numbers." Pause. "What result did you get?"

Joyce says, "Fifteen." You turn the sheet over, showing that you correctly predicted the result.

If you examine the original layout, you will see that the answer will always be 15. Take a number in the first row and add it to a number in the second row which is not in the same column. To this add the number in the third row which is not in either of the previously chosen columns. The result is always 15.

That's why you don't want them examining your layout. Ball up the sheet of paper and stick it into your purse or pocket.

"Let's make it more difficult." This time you write the number 34 on one side of a fresh sheet of paper, making sure no one can see what you write. Turn the paper over, and construct a 4 × 4 grid containing numbers 1 to 16, as shown in Illus. 16.

1	2	3	4
5	6	7	8
9	10	11	12
13	14	15	16

Illus. 16

Following the same procedure as before, Joyce circles *four* numbers. When they are added up, the total is 34. You show your prediction, ball up the paper, put it away, and proceed with your next demonstration.

Hint of Mystery

Now you will try to fathom a spectator's thoughts, using written numbers to assist you.

With your back turned, ask Patsy to write down any three-digit number, using three *different* digits. Then provide these directions, with appropriate pauses: "Write down the same three digits, only in reverse order. Subtract the smaller number from the larger."

After some concentration, say, "You have a three-digit number, right?"

If Patsy answers no, the correct number is 99. After further thought, you can reveal this, and the trick is over.

Usually, however, it will be a three-digit number. And the *middle* digit is always 9. What's more, the end digits will always *total* 9. "I'm just not getting the number, Patsy," you say. "Maybe I can get it with a little hint. Will you please give me either your first or last digit. Which would you prefer to give me, the first or the last?"

Let's assume that she gives you the last digit and that it is 6. You already know that the middle digit is 9. The first and last digits total 9, so you subtract 6—the last digit—from 9, getting 3. So the first digit is 3. And the entire number is 396.

Naturally, you reveal this gradually, as the thought waves arrive bit by bit.

Let's try an example. Patsy writes down 459. She reverses the digits and writes down 954. She subtracts the lower number from the higher number.

$$
\begin{array}{r}
954 \\
-459 \\
\hline
495
\end{array}
$$

You suggest that she has a three-digit number. She agrees. You ask for a hint; she tells you the first digit is a 4. Since the first and last digits always total 9, you know that the last digit must be 5. The middle digit is always 9, so you know that the number must be 495.

The trick may be repeated, provided that the first number arrived at is *not* 99. You don't want to take the chance of getting 99 twice in a row.

A Random Choice

Fitch Cheney developed this trick, which I have refined somewhat.

Hand Ellen a pen and paper, saying, "Ellen, I'm going to try to read your mind. First, we must have you take a number at random. In a moment, I'll explain how you do this. Then we must have the number written down so that the mental image will be more concrete. To start, do you prefer odd numbers, like 3, 5, and 7, or even numbers, like 2, 4, and 6?"

Suppose she chooses odd numbers. Say, "Fine, we'll use odd numbers then. Now, if you want to change your mind, you may." She doesn't want to. "Excellent! I prefer odd numbers."

It doesn't matter if she chooses even numbers, since either odd or even numbers will work.

Turn away, saying, "I don't want to see any of your numbers. Actually, I *do* want to see your numbers, but that wouldn't be quite fair. Now, Ellen, I'd like you to write down any four odd numbers that are in succession. For instance, you could write 13, 15, 17, 19." When she finishes, continue. "Now multiply the largest number by the smallest number." Wait. "Have you done that? Good. Now to make sure that you end up with a completely random number, let's add a digit to that total. Name a number from 1 to 9." She does so. "Excellent. Just add that to your result."

Pause. "Now circle your result, please. Remember the four numbers you wrote down at the beginning, Ellen? You multiplied the highest and lowest numbers, right? Now please multiply the other two numbers." When she's ready, continue: "Let's add something to *that* total also. Name another digit from 1 to 9." She does so. "Add that to the total you got when you multiplied the middle numbers."

Pause. "Let's see. Oh, yes, put a circle around your last result. Now, you have two circled numbers. Please subtract the smaller from the larger."

Pause. "Now *that* result is your final number. And it's about as random as you can get. Please concentrate on your number, Ellen."

As usual, the dark clouds finally clear away, and you come up with the correct number.

Here's how it works: Write down four consecutive odd numbers or four consecutive even numbers. Multiply the largest and the smallest. Multiply the two middle numbers. Subtract the smaller from the larger. The result is always 8. For instance, suppose you write down 8, 10, 12, 14. You multiply 8 by 14, getting 112. You multiply 10 by 12, getting 120. You subtract 112 from 120, getting 8. You *always* get 8.

My contribution is to provide window-dressing so that you *don't* always get 8, but still know the answer. This enables you to repeat the stunt if you desire.

After Ellen did the first multiplication, you told her to name a digit and add it to her total. Let's suppose she named 6. Whatever number she names, you subtract it from 8. In the example, she named 6. 8 minus 6 = 2. So you remember 2. After the next multiplication, she names another digit—3, for instance. You *add* this to the number you're remembering, 2. 2 + 3 = 5. And 5 is the number she ends up with.

Let's take another example to illustrate the lone exception. Ellen writes down 30, 32, 34, 36. She multiplies 30 by 36, getting 1080. You tell her to name a digit and add it to her result. She names 9 and adds it to her result, getting 1089. But you are to subtract the digit she chooses from 8. So when you subtract 9 from 8, you get minus 1. Remember the −1.

Now she multiplies the two middle numbers and gets 1088. Again she names a digit—6, for instance—and adds it to her result, getting 1094. You add 6 to the −1, getting 5. She subtracts 1089 from 1094, and gets 5.

Review

(1) Spectator writes four consecutive numbers, either odd or even.

(2) She multiplies the two largest numbers.

(3) She names a digit and adds it to her result, which she circles. (You subtract the number she names from 8, and remember the result. If she names 5, for instance, you subtract 5 from 8 and remember 3. If she should choose 9, remember −1.)

(4) She multiplies the two middle numbers.

(5) She names another digit and adds it to the result of multiplying the two middle numbers. She circles this result. (You add the number she names to the digit you're remembering. Suppose she names the digit 7; you add this to the number you're remembering—in this example, 3. The result is 10.)

(6) She subtracts the smaller circled number from the larger. (In this instance, she ends up with 10, which you announce.)

Note: If you repeat the trick, get rid of the sheet on which she did her figuring. Provide a new sheet, saying, "We'll need a clean sheet." Also, on a repeat, it would be best to work with a different spectator.

And Nothing Remains

Needed: Pen, paper, several coins in one pocket, and a likely spectator—Jack, for instance.

Hand Jack a pen and paper and then turn away. Ask him to think of any three-digit number and then to write it down. Continue, with appropriate pauses: "Now repeat that three-digit number so that then you have a six-digit number. For instance, if you chose 583, write down 583 again, so that your number would be 583583. Now divide that number by 7. Take your time."

When Jack announces that he is finished, ask him to check his math. "For me to perform this mental miracle, the math must be *absolutely* correct."

When he is done, continue: "Now please pass the paper around so that everyone can see what you've done." Pause. "Please don't say a word, Jack, because I want you to note the remainder and remember it. Now hide the math work so I can't possibly see it."

Turn back and, with your left hand, remove a fairly large number of coins from a left pocket—let's say seven or more coins. Place both hands together and rattle the coins as loud as you can in your hands (Illus. 17). "I hope you remember the remainder, Jack, because I'm going to match that exact number."

Illus. 17

Illus. 18

Turn your hands so that the left hand is palm up. With a grasping motion of your right hand, pretend to take some coins from the left hand (Illus. 18). Actually, you take *none*. Then, move your right hand away in a fist and, as the right hand clears the left fingers, close this hand into a fist also (Illus. 19).

Hold up the right fist, announcing triumphantly, "Here I have a number of coins equal to the remainder."

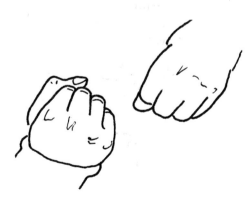

Illus. 19

Hold both hands in a loose fist. Bring the fists together, side by side, as you raise them in front of you, backs to the audience (Illus. 20). Still holding the fists together, shake them, rattling the coins in the left hand. Put the coins that are in your left hand back into the left pocket.

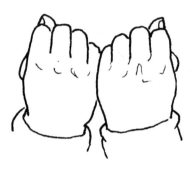

Illus. 20

Hold up your right hand. "Does anyone here doubt my mental powers? Does anyone think I could *possibly* be wrong?" Here you overact a bit, so that spectators will know you're not really an arrogant dolt. "I can assure you that I *never* miss. (Quietly) Well, hardly ever."

Many in the group will be certain you are wrong, because *there is no remainder*. And, of course, when you open your right hand, it holds no coins.

This trick is based on a little-known mathematical principle: When a six-figured number is developed as above, there is never a remainder.

BRAIN POWER

In these tricks, you display your mental prowess and agility. You are a memory expert, a lightning calculator, a veritable mathematical genius. With all of these, you will need pen and paper.

It All Adds Up

People won't believe how fast you can do addition. It's positively amazing! You demonstrate your astonishing ability by means of an old trick. My handling, I believe, puts spark back into the trick, and makes it much more convincing.

On the table, you have a pen and paper. Introduce the trick by saying, "I'd like to attempt an experiment in lightning calculation. I've been practicing a great deal, and I rarely miss by more than a number or two. But let's put it to the test."

Ask Herb to write down a five-digit number on the paper. Point to a spot about a quarter of the way down the sheet. Suppose Herb puts down this number: 58392 (Illus. 21).

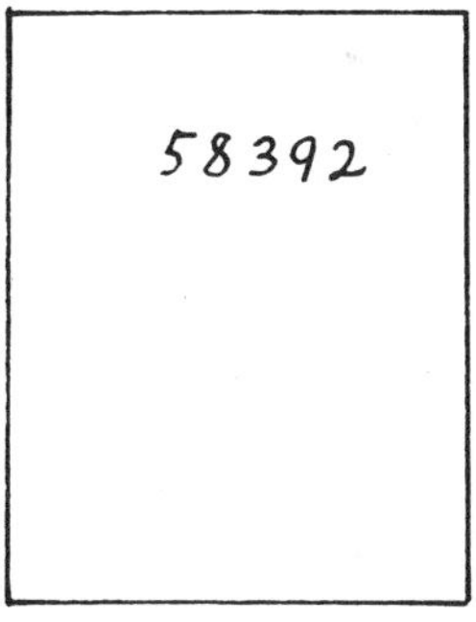

Illus. 21

61

Ask Rudy to help out. "Rudy, I'd like you to also write down a five-figured number. Put it here, please." Point to a spot about an inch below the first number. Let's suppose Rudy puts down this number: 96451. The paper will look like Illus. 22.

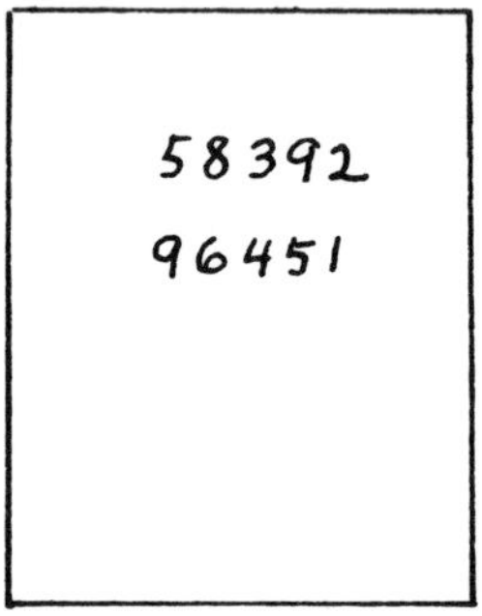

58392
96451

Illus. 22

Now comes the sneaky part. You say, "I'll put in a few numbers, just to make things more confusing." Ha! It's *your* numbers that make the trick work. You take a look at the second number, 96451. The first number you write will make each digit of this number equal 9. Your intention is to write a five-digit number. But the first digit of Rudy's number is 9, so you put no digit in the first position; you will have only a four-digit number. Rudy's second digit is 6. Subtract this from 9 and you get 3. This is the first digit you write down.

The third digit is 4; subtract this from 9, and you get 5—the second digit you write down.

The fourth digit is 5; subtract this from 9, and you get 4—the third digit you write down.

The last digit is 1; subtract this from 9, and you get 8—the last digit you write down.

So the number you write down is 3548. And you write this, as you compute it, *above* the first number written down (Illus. 23).

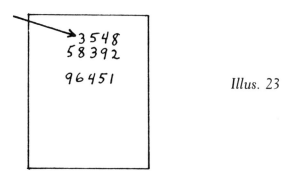

Illus. 23

The second number you write down is based on Herb's number, 58392. Subtracting each digit from 9, you get 41607. You place this, as you compute it, *below* the last number written down (Illus. 24).

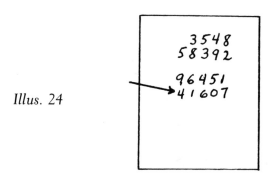

Illus. 24

Unlike other versions of this trick, all is done quite openly. Note that there is a space in the middle. It is time for Charlotte to help out. "Charlotte, would you place a five-digit number right here." Point to the space in the middle. Charlotte does so. Suppose she writes 83974. The sheet now looks like Illus. 25.

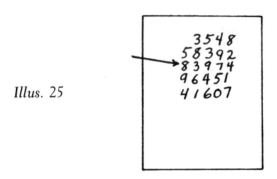

Illus. 25

As soon as she finishes writing, take the pen from her, draw a line under the bottom number, and put a plus sign next to the column of numbers. Take a quick look at the paper, saying, "Let me work this out now." Write down your calculation at the bottom of the sheet, shielding your number with your other hand. Tear off the bottom quarter of the sheet, and place it face down upon the table.

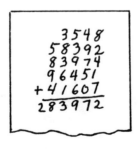

Illus. 26

"Charlotte, please add up the numbers and announce the total." She does so. You repeat the total, and then turn your prediction over, showing that you calculated the result perfectly in mere seconds.

How in the world did you do that?

When you took that quick look at the paper, you noted Charlotte's number, the one in the middle. You wrote this number down, placing a 2 in front of it, and subtracting 2 from the last digit. Charlotte's number was 83974. You placed a 2 in front of it and subtracted 2 from the 4 at the end, giving you 283972. This is the result Charlotte got when she added the numbers (Illus. 26).

Notes

1. To be on the safe side, don't let anyone study the sheet with the numbers on it. After you've shown that the numbers match, wad up the papers and stick them in your pocket or purse. Immediately go into your next demonstration.

2. Once in a while, a spectator will write a number in the middle which ends in 1 or a 0. Clearly, you cannot subtract 2 from this. So you simply subtract 2 from the last *two* digits. For instance, if Charlotte had written 83970, you would put a 2 in front of it when you wrote your prediction. But since you cannot subtract 2 from 0, you subtract 2 from the last two digits, 70. 70 minus 2 is 68. So your last *two* digits will be 68. The entire prediction would then be 283968.

An Additional Feat

Larry White developed a superb prediction trick called "The Power of Five." As far as I know, the principle was new. In his trick, White used the digits 1 through 5. In my version, the spectator *chooses* any five digits, from 1 through 9. My discovery of an intriguing math principle made this possible. Further, although my version *can* be used as a prediction, I prefer to present it as "lightning calculation."

One outstanding feature of White's trick is strong spectator participation; this has been retained. You can use up to five spectators. Needed are a deck of cards, pen, and paper.

Let's assume you have two volunteers, Ida and Bud. Explain: "I would like to offer a demonstration of lightning calculation— adding up numbers at an almost impossible speed. Obviously, we must make sure we choose numbers at random."

Hand the deck to Ida, saying, "I'd like you to remove from the deck five sets of cards. You're to remove cards from ace to nine. They are to stand for the digits from 1 to 9. For example, you might remove all the threes, all the fives, all the sixes, all the sevens, and all the nines. It doesn't matter which sets you remove, as long as there are no tens or face cards."

Help Ida as she removes the five sets. Take these cards from her and have her set the rest of the deck aside. Take one set of four-of-a-kind and hand them to Ida, saying, "Would you please place these four cards in a row on the table." After she does so, hand her another set of four of a kind, asking her to deal these on top of the first four. Do the same with the other three sets of four."

Sitting on the table are *four sets* of *five cards*. The piles all contain one card of each value removed from the deck. For instance, if Ida removed aces, threes, fours, sixes, and sevens from the deck, each pile would contain an ace, 3, 4, 6, and 7.

As the cards are distributed, you must total the chosen values. In the example, Ida chose A, 3, 4, 6, and 7. You add these together: $1 + 3 + 4 + 6 + 7 = 21$. You must remember the total, 21, which becomes your *key number*.

Have both spectators shuffle *each* pile separately. "Bud, in a moment, you are going to form the numbers by turning over the top card of each pile and setting it face up in front of the pile." Indicate where the cards are to be placed. Hand Ida the pen and paper. "Ida, each card that is turned up will represent a digit. I would like you to enter those digits on the paper as a four-digit number."

Make sure that everything is clear. "Now I'll turn my back, and we can begin." Turn away. After the first number is entered, say, "Bud, I'd like you to turn over the top card of each pile and set it face up on the first card you turned over. Ida, write down this four-digit number below the first number."

Have the procedure repeated three more times. Bud is out of cards, and Ida has written down five four-digit numbers in a column.

Turn back to the group, but make it obvious that you are not looking at the paper or the face-up cards.

"We should now have five numbers with four digits in each number. Is that right, Ida?" Of course. "Clearly, these numbers were chosen at random, so there is no way I could know their order, much less what they total. So, I'm now going to add them up—in seconds!"

Tell Ida to draw a line under the numbers. Take the pen from her and turn the paper so that you can see the numbers. Rapidly write the correct total below the line.

What number do you put in? In the example, you added up the five values chosen and came up with 21, your *key number*. The answer, then, would be 23331, which you should write as 23,331. The first digit is the first digit of your *key number*. The last digit is the second digit of your *key number*. The three middle digits are the same—the total of the first and second digits of your *key number*. (There are three exceptions, which I will explain later.)

When you write your answer, make sure you put in the comma after the first two digits; this tends to disguise the fact that the middle three digits are identical.

Let's try another example. Suppose the chosen values are 2, 4, 5, 6, and 9. You add them up: $2 + 4 + 5 + 6 + 9 = 26$. So 26 is your *key number*. At this point, you know that the answer will be 28,886. 2 and 6 are the first and last digits respectively, and the sum of these two makes up the three middle digits.

Why does this work? Suppose the chosen values are 2, 3, 4, 6, and 9. Each of the four piles contains a set of these values. Each pile is shuffled so that the five cards are distributed randomly. Let's see what happens:

	PILE A	PILE B	PILE C	PILE D
1st CARD	2	9	6	3
2nd CARD	9	4	2	4
3rd CARD	3	6	9	2
4th CARD	4	3	3	6
5th CARD	6	2	4	9

Notice that one card of each value is in each column. It doesn't matter what order the cards are in, because each column will always add up to the same total. Therefore, any specific group of five values will always produce the same answer.

Let's add up the above values:

$$2963$$
$$9424$$
$$3692$$
$$4336$$
$$\underline{6249}$$
$$26,664$$

But you already knew that. You added up the values—2, 3, 4, 6, 9—and you got your *key number*, 24. The answer is 26,664. The first digit is the same as the first digit of your *key number*.

The last digit is the second digit of your *key number*. Each of the middle three digits is the same—the total of the first and second digits of your *key number*.

After you have done your rapid calculation, have either Ida or Bud check the answer by adding up the figures. To emphasize the magnitude of your feat, choose the one who seems least likely to have math ability.

As I told you, there are three exceptions to the method of figuring the answer. Since there are 21 possible *key numbers*, this means that, on the average, one time in seven you'll have to do a bit more math.

The exceptions are the numbers 19, 28, and 29. Immediately you will see that when you try to add the two digits, you end up with *another* two-digit number. So you do not have the three middle digits for your answer. If you wanted to, you could memorize the appropriate answers for 19, 28, and 29. For 19, the answer is 21,109; for 28, it is 31,108; for 29, it is 32,219. But I have worked out an easier method.

Let's say that the *key number* is 19. Take a quick glance at the sheet and say, "Oh, I think I know that answer." Below the line, quickly jot down *from left to right* the answer to the *key number before* 19, which of course is 18. So, below the line, you write 19,998. Make no big point of it, but shield your answer so others can't see it. Take a quick glance at your answer. "Oh, no! That's completely wrong. I'll have to actually add it up."

Quickly put in the correct answer, moving from *right to left*. What you actually do is mentally add 1111 as you move from right to left. 19,998 + 1111 = 21,109, which is the correct answer. As you mentally add the 1111, first add in the number you're carrying and then add the 1 from 1111.

In the same way, when your *key number* is 28, work out the answer to the previous number, 27: 29,997. Jot this down first and then notice your mistake. Once more, add 1111.

When the *key number* is 29, however, you must work out the answer to 27 and then add 2222. Clearly, this is only slightly more difficult than adding 1111.

In all instances, thoroughly scratch out your "rough guess" before letting anyone else see the sheet.

Notes

(1) Since the calculation is so easy, you might choose to write in your answer from *right to left*, creating the illusion that you are adding up the digits in normal fashion, but doing it at unbelievable speed. So, as you work from right to left, quickly glance at each column before you write the digit down. Do *not* diminish your speed, of course.

And, as you go from right to left, be sure to insert the *comma* where it belongs. As I mentioned, the comma tends to conceal the fact that the three middle numbers are identical.

(2) You can perform the trick for one person by having her perform all the duties. Similarly, you can assign duties to three or four spectators.

If the group is large enough, five spectators can participate. Spectator 1 will take out the five sets of four-of-a-kind. Have the other four spectators stand side by side so that both the audience and Spectator 1 can see them as they display their cards. Give Spectator 1 a set of four-of-a-kind, and direct him to give one to each of the other four helpers. This is repeated four times. Spectators 2 to 5 shuffle their packets and, after you turn your back, display their top card. Tell Spectator 1 to write down the four-digit number, adding, "After you write it down, take the four cards that are being shown and set them aside face down." Be sure to repeat this last instruction each time the spectators display their cards. Proceed to the conclusion as described above.

(3) If you choose to do the trick as a prediction, simply write the prediction immediately after you total up the values, saying, "Oh, I almost forgot to write my prediction." The patter should then deal with forecasting the future, rather than lightning calculation.

(4) Because of the similarity of the answers, it's best not to repeat the trick. But if you must, wait until later in your presen-

tation. And before you repeat it, get rid of the sheet containing the original numbers.

Divide and Concur

How about another demonstration of your mathematical wizardry? This one is probably the easiest of all, and, oddly enough, one of the most effective. You will of course need pen and paper.

"Like most people," you announce, "I cannot do short division really rapidly. But I do have a subconscious gift. Although it isn't a really useful gift, I'm grateful for whatever gifts I have. The gift is this: I can look at a long string of numbers and tell immediately whether it can be evenly divided by 4. In other words, can it be divided by 4 with no remainder?"

Since Sonja is good with numbers, hand her the pen and paper, saying, "I'd like you to write down a fairly long number. Make it at least eight digits, but you can make it as many as you wish. But take it a little easy on yourself. Eventually, you're going to have to divide your number by 4. I'll turn away while you write your number down."

Turn away. When Sonja is done, take the paper and look at the last two digits of her number. If you're very lucky, the last two digits will form a number which can be divided evenly by 4. For example, she may have written this:

651708236948

The last two digits, 48, can be evenly divided by 4. So you hand the paper back to Sonja, saying, "Oh, yes. This number can be divided evenly by 4. When you divide it by 4, there'll be no remainder. Would you check that, please?"

When she divides the number by 4, there is no remainder.

Suppose, however, that Sonja writes a number in which the last two digits are *not* evenly divisible by 4. (This, by the way, is far more likely.) You say, "No, Sonja, this number cannot be evenly divided by 4. But I can fix it so it will be."

You add two digits to the end of the number and hand the paper back to Sonja for her to perform the short division process. You probably have already guessed the nature of those two digits you added. That's right. They are two digits that are divisible by 4. You can use any two digits that can be divided by 4: 12, 16, 20, 24, 28, 32, 36, 40, 44, 48, 52, and so on.

When Sonja finishes her short division, she will find that you indeed made the number evenly divisible by 4.

You can perform the stunt a number of times. But when you add those two digits to the end of the number, remember to make them different each time.

Any Which Way

Any number of persons, magicians and others, have invented "magic squares." As far as I am concerned, David Altman came up with the best one for use in a performance. Unlike similar squares, it is easy to construct. What's more, it produces an extraordinary trick.

You will need a writing instrument and a sheet of paper. On the paper is a 4×4 grid (Illus. 27). This need not be perfect; frequently, in an impromptu performance, I have dashed one off freehand.

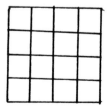

Illus. 27

Say to a spectator, "Give me a number between 30 and 100. This will become your lucky number, as you'll see." After you're given the number, explain, "Now I'm going to construct a Magic Square based on your number."

Suppose the spectator gives you the number 57. Write this down to one side on your paper; this will help with your computations. Now fill in the squares.

Row One: Subtract 3 from the first digit of the spectator's chosen number. In this instance, you subtract 3 from 5, getting 2. Write down 2 as the first number in Row One. Put the consecutive numbers in the remaining three boxes (Illus. 28).

Illus. 28

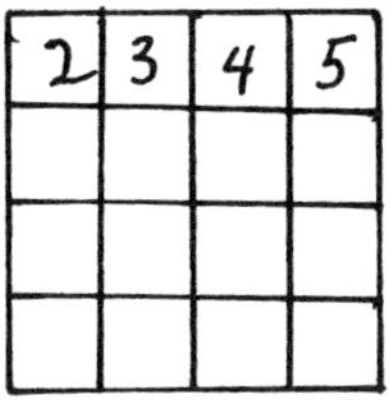

Next, you derive a *key number*, to be used in the remaining three rows. The spectator's chosen number is 57. The *key number* is simply the first digit of this number plus 1. Here, the spectator's first digit is 5; add 1 to it and you get 6—your *key number*.

Row Two: To the *key number*, add the first number in Row One. The *key number* is 6. Add 2 to this, and you get 8. Put 8 down in the first box in row 2. Fill the row with consecutive numbers (Illus. 29).

Illus. 29

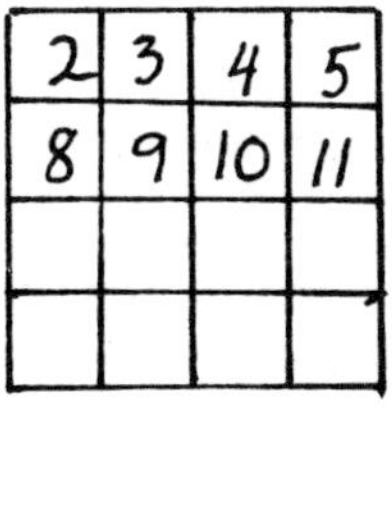

Row Three: This is similar to the development of Row Two. To the *key number*, add the first number in Row Two. The *key number* is 6. Add 8 to this, and you get 14. Put 14 down in the first box in Row Three. Fill the row with consecutive numbers (Illus. 30).

2	3	4	5
8	9	10	11
14	15	16	17

Row Four: As with Rows Two and Three, you begin by adding the *key number* to the first number in the previous row. So we add 6, the *key number*, to 14, the first number in Row Three. The result is 20.

Now, for the first time, the second digit of the spectator's number comes into play. The chosen number was 57; obviously, the second digit is 7. Add this to your previous result: 7 + 20 = 27. This gives you the first number in Row Four. The row is filled out with consecutive numbers (Illus. 31).

2	3	4	5
8	9	10	11
14	15	16	17
27	28	29	30

Illus. 31

After you construct your Magic Square, say to the spectator, "Don't forget that your number was 57. Now I want you to pick out four numbers, but no two numbers can be in the same row or column. Just circle the numbers you pick."
The spectator might circle the numbers as in Illus. 32.

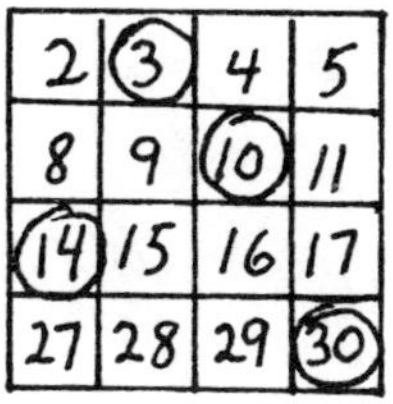

Illus. 32

"Please add up the numbers you picked." The numbers total his original number, 57.
Incidentally, if the spectator does not understand your instructions, have him circle a number, and then cross out all the other numbers in that row and column (Illus. 33).

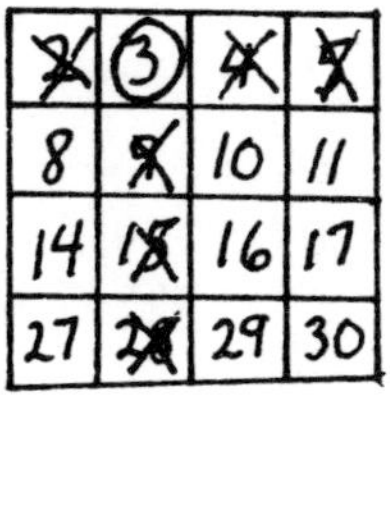

Illus. 33

He does this twice more. Three numbers are circled, and all the rest are crossed out, except one. This remaining number is also circled (Illus. 34). Notice that in the illustration, these circled numbers also add up to 57. If the Magic Square is properly constructed, the total will always be the same as the spectator's chosen number.

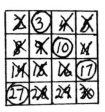

Illus. 34

If the group is interested, you should be happy to repeat the stunt.

Review

A spectator chooses a number between 30 and 100. You jot this down on your paper as a reminder. Then you construct your Magic Square.

Row One: Subtract 3 from the first digit of the spectator's chosen number. Enter the result in the first square. Other numbers are consecutive.

Row Two: Derive a *key number* by adding 1 to the first digit of the chosen number. To this *key number* add the number in the first box in Row One. Enter this in the first square of Row Two. Other numbers are consecutive.

Row Three: To the *key number* add the number in the first box in Row Two. Enter this in the first square of Row Three. Other numbers are consecutive.

Row Four: To the *key number* add the number in the first box in Row Three. To this result add the spectator's *second digit*. This gives you the first number in Row Four. Other numbers are consecutive.

The Memory Expert

In real estate, the three important things are location, location, location. In magic, it's presentation, presentation, presentation. A case in point is this trick shown to me by Milt Kort. All that happens is that a card is forced on a spectator, and the magician finds the card. But see how it looks when you dress it up in pretty clothes.

If you happen to know a good method of forcing a card on a spectator, then use that one. Otherwise, you might as well use the crisscross force, which is easy to do, fools spectators, and is particularly appropriate for a mental effect. Secretly get a peek at the top card. (You might sneak a look at the bottom card and bring it to the top with an overhand shuffle.) Then set the deck on the table and say to Clare, "I'd like you to help me out with an experiment, Clare. Would you please cut off about half the cards and set them on the table." After she does so, pick up the bottom half of the deck and place it crosswise on the other packet (Illus. 35).

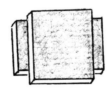

Illus. 35

"In a moment," you say, "I am going to attempt to memorize the position of every card in the deck. Sometimes it works; sometimes it doesn't. It depends on how well I concentrate. But before I do this, I need to have a card chosen. Clare, would you please look at the card you cut to." As you say this, *touch* the card on top of the lower pile on the table. It is, of course, the card you peeked at earlier. Avert your head and say, "Show the card around, please." When she is done, say, "Now put the card in the deck somewhere and give the deck a good shuffle."

Take the deck from Clare and spread the cards out face up on the table. Move the cards with your fingers so that the face of every card can be seen. "Now I'm going to try to memorize the deck." Very slowly move your hand from one end of the deck to the other, following along with your eyes as you study every card. Actually, you are looking for the card you forced. When you see it, note the name of one of the cards next to it.

Close your eyes for a moment as you draw a few deep breaths. "All right, I think I've got it. When I turn my back, Clare, I'd like you to slide out your card from its present position and place it in some other position in the deck." Make sure she understands what she is to do. Turn your back.

When Clare announces that she is done, turn back. Again, starting at one end, slowly study the cards, following the movement of your hand. When you come to the card which was next to the one you forced, stop. Tap that card with your hand. "Right around here somewhere a card is missing. I can't tell which one; I just know that the order has been disturbed."

Move your hand along the spread of cards until you come to the chosen one. Stare at the cards in that area. "One of these doesn't belong here." Study the cards further. Let your hand drop onto the chosen card. "This one. This is the card you moved— your chosen card. Is that right?"

Of course it is. Gather up the cards and give them a shuffle. If you're requested to repeat the experiment, explain, "The cards are all mixed up now. I can't concentrate enough to do it again. Perhaps another time."

Amazing Writing

Bill Elliott discovered an easy way to show your skill with numbers. Although the task seems difficult, many will find they can perform the feat the first time they try it. And virtually everyone can learn the trick with a bit of practice.

You need pen and paper. Address the group: "I've been practicing for many years and finally have mastered an almost impossible feat." Pick up the pen. "It's extremely easy to jot down the digits in order while you say them."

Recite the digits 1 to 9 aloud as you write them down.

"It's also pretty easy to write the digits backwards as you say them backwards."

Write the digits in reverse order, naming each as you do so.

"However, it's fairly hard to say the digits in the correct order as you write them down in reverse order."

Do so.

"And it's absolutely impossible to say them in their proper order while writing them in reverse order—*upside down!*"

Do so, and then take a bow. If possible, do not let anyone else attempt it. Instead, swing right into another trick.

When you first attempt the upside-down writing, you may find that you proceed fairly slowly. After several tries, you'll find that you can write the digits down quite rapidly.

There is really no trick at all to reciting the digits forward as you write them backwards. Habit permits us to recite them by rote as we perform another task.

FUN WITH MENTALISM

The Screwball Clock

All you need for this amusing and deceptive trick is a sheet of paper and a pen.

"One of my many crazy relatives is a clockmaker—my Uncle Loony. For my last birthday, he gave me a clock. I'll draw a picture of it for you."

Illus. 36

Place a sheet of paper on the table. Draw a big circle on it. Inside the circle, write the numbers 1 to 12 in varied sizes as you place them in random order (Illus. 36). Hold the sheet up so that all can see it, saying, "There it is—a picture of my screwball clock, presented to me by my beloved Uncle Loony. All the times are on the clock, but they're scattered all over the place. But the clock would be useless anyway, since there are no hands on it. I told this to my Uncle Loony, but he said to me, 'Listen carefully, my dear dense nephew: If you do it just right, you can actually read someone's mind with this clock.' And then he told me how. So let's see if it works."

Address Duane: "Duane, I'd like you to think of any one of these times—from one to twelve." When he has thought of one, continue: "Duane, I want you to concentrate on your time. I'm going to tap on this paper over different numbers, one at a time. Every time I tap, I want you to add one to the time you thought of. For example, let's say the number you thought of is 6. When I tap once, you would think of 7. When I tap again, you would think of 8. And so on. When I tap and you're thinking of the number 20, tell me to stop." Make sure he understands.

Begin tapping with the pen on different numbers. Do this slowly, so that Duane doesn't lose track. Your first *seven* taps are on random numbers, but when you make the eighth tap, rap the pen on number 12. The next number you tap is 11. Continue with this backward sequence, tapping 10, 9, 8, etc., until Duane tells you to stop. When he says stop, your pen will be resting on his number.

"Do you see the number my pen is on, Duane?" He does. "Is this your number?" Yes, it is.

"Let's make it more difficult." Address Amy: "Amy, I'd like you to simply think of any number from 15 to 25. Do you have one? What is the number you have chosen?" She names it. Turn to Duane, "This time, Duane, I'd like you to think of any number on the screwball clock. As before, each time I tap, I'd like you to add one to the number you're thinking of. When we hit the number Amy named, tell me to stop."

Again, make sure Duane understands the instructions.

Here's what you do: Subtract 12 from the number Amy has given. Suppose Amy has selected 18. Subtract 12 from 18 and you have 6. As you tap, hit five different numbers at random. At 6, make sure you tap the number 12. Continue tapping backwards in sequence—11, 10, 9, etc. When you are told to stop, again your pen is resting on the chosen number.

Suppose Amy has chosen the number 21. Subtract 12 from 21, giving you 9. Make sure that the ninth number you tap is 12. Continue with the backward sequence, tapping 11, 10, 9, etc. in order. As before, when Duane says stop, the pen is resting on the chosen number.

Note: If pen and paper are not available, you can perform the same stunt with playing cards. Remove from the deck any A 2 3 4 5 6 7 8 9 10 J Q sequence. Spread them out in a screwball clock, explaining that the jack is 11 and the queen is 12. Use your finger as the tapper, and follow the exact procedure described above.

Why do we use a "screwball clock" for this trick? To make it difficult for spectators to tell that you are tapping the last several numbers in a backward sequence.

Happy Birthday

I was sixteen years old, attending a carnival in Chelsea, Michigan. A slight, middle-aged lady approached me. Since she wore a bandanna and a long, colorful dress, I assumed she was a Gypsy, or a facsimile.

"What year were you born in?" she asked me.

I told her.

"I thought so," she said. "I'll bet you a quarter I can tell you within four days the day you were born."

"Okay."

She held out her hand; I placed a quarter in it.

"Wednesday," she said, and walked off.

The Invisible Dice

Milt Kort showed me this trick. You will need paper, a pen, and two "invisible" dice.

Reach into your pocket and pretend to remove a pair of dice. Hold them up for inspection. "As you can see, I have a pair of dice here. I recently bought them from a stranger who said they'd bring me good luck. Some people *claim* they can't see the dice. Of course, some people claim they can't see me either."

Roll the dice out on the table several times, demonstrating that different numbers come up each time. "Notice that the dice are not loaded and, in fact, are ordinary in every way. Alfred, you can see the dice, can't you?" Alfred usually goes along with a gag, so he probably will say yes. (If not, you can try someone else.) "While my back is turned, Alfred, I'd like you to roll the dice."

Turn away. Alfred rolls the invisible dice. "Do you see the two numbers you rolled?" Yes, he does. "I can't seem to get a picture of your numbers. I put paper and a pen on the table. Please write your two digits down."

Proceed with appropriate pauses: "Circle the larger of the two digits. If both digits are the same, just circle one of them. Double the number that you circled. Add five to it. Multiply the result by five. Add to that result the smaller digit that you rolled. What did you get?"

Alfred tells you. "Hide the paper so I can't see it." Turn back to the group. Mentally subtract 25 from the number Alfred gave you; this gives you the two digits he rolled.

For instance, Alfred says his result is 88. You subtract 25, giving you 63. You declare, "The two numbers you rolled are six and three, right?"

Alfred agrees.

"Do you know how I knew?" Alfred will probably say no. If he tries an explanation, interrupt him, saying, "No, Alfred. You left the dice right here on the table." Pick up the invisible dice and put them away.

Note: When working with invisible objects, be sure to treat them exactly as though they were real. With dice, for instance, shake them and roll them as though they really existed. Perhaps one die rolls off the table to the floor. Stoop down, pick it up, roll it again. Add little touches to sell the idea that they exist. As a result, two things happen: People are amused, and, fleetingly, they suspend their disbelief.

Prediction by Hand

Again, I am indebted to Milt Kort for sharing this with me.

You will need pen and paper, along with two assistants from the group. Perhaps Anita and Harold will be kind enough to help.

Ask Anita to hold out one of her hands palm up. Pretend to remove something from your pocket with your right hand. Hold up your hand as though holding something in it. The audience should see the view as in Illus. 37.

Illus. 37

"I am about to make a prediction. And I want the prediction to be in your hand, Anita." Reach over with your right hand, pretending to place something on Anita's palm. Actually, you

Illus. 38

merely press hard with your middle fingernails into her palm (Illus. 38). Immediately say, "Right now, please close your hand into a tight fist." Withdraw your fingers as she does so. "Continue holding that fist closed, please . . . because right there in your hand, you have my prediction."
Turn to Harold. "Are you good at math, Harold?" Whatever he answers, continue: "Well, this should be pretty easy." Have him take the pen and paper. "While I turn away, I'd like you to jot down the digits in a memorable date. If you were married on April 19, for instance, you might jot down the number 19. If you were born on the seventh day of a month, you might jot down the number 7." Turn away.
Harold writes down his number. Let's suppose he jots down 12.
"Is your number written down? Good. I'll bet that the day after that was also memorable, so jot down that number below your original number. For instance, if your original number was 6, you would jot down the number 7."
Harold jots down 13 below the 12.
"Add those two numbers together."
He adds 13 and 12, getting 25.
"Add 9 to the result."
Harold adds 9, getting 34.
"Divide that result by 2."
He divides 34 by 2, getting 17.
"Remember your original number, the one that was a special day? Please subtract that number."

Harold remembers that his original number was 12. He subtracts that, getting 5. (He will *always* get 5.)

"Hide your paper so that I can't see it."

Turn back to the group and address Anita: "In your hand, Anita, you have my prediction. Please open your hand." She opens her hand and probably looks puzzled. "How many do you have?" If she is still puzzled, count her digits for her, touching each one as you do so: "One, two, three, four, five. The number is 5. And what number did you end up with, Harold?"

He also has 5. Your prediction is right on the mark.

Summary

(1) Think of a memorable date and write down the one or two digits that represent that date.

(2) The next day was probably also memorable, so write down that date below the first one.

(3) Add the two dates.

(4) Add 9 to the result.

(5) Divide by 2.

(6) Subtract the number representing the original date.

The result is always 5.

MISCELLANEOUS

This section contains miscellaneous mental tricks which include some of the best in the book. We start with two totally impromptu tricks, requiring no materials whatsoever.

Probably Hungry or Angry

The basic idea was created by Michael Carpenter, Sr. from a piece of trivia he once heard. It is an astonishing quickie, which I have filled out a bit.

"I've been working very hard trying to develop my telepathic ability. Sometimes I do very well, and sometimes I fall flat on my subconscious." Turn to Victor. "I wonder if you'd share an experiment with me, Victor." He agrees. "Sometimes it helps to warm up with something really tough, to sort of check out the thought waves. This may not work, Victor, but it might help to put our minds in tune. Would you please think of a word—not a name—that ends in the letters B-L-Y."

You are hoping that he will think of the word "probably," but it won't matter much if he doesn't. Feigning deep concentration, you say, "I see the letter R in the word. Is there an R?" If there is, go for it, and say, "It's not very clear, but I think the word might be *probably*. Is that right?" If so, proceed with the next step. If there is no R in the word, or if "probably" is incorrect, say, "Yes, it wasn't very clear. But possibly we're getting more in tune."

Whether you get the word or not, proceed: "This time, Victor, I'd like you to think of a word ending in . . . Oh, I don't know . . . How about a word ending in the letters G-R-Y?" Again you strain your mind. "Victor, I see the letter A. Is the letter A in your word?" If it is, say, "I thought so. That's more like it. Your word is . . . *angry*."

Suppose the letter A is not in his word. Close your eyes and say, "Of course not. I can see it now . . . The two letters are very similar . . . It's not a capital A, it's a capital H. Your word is *hungry*."

Angry and *hungry* are the only common words I know of that end in *gry*.

If *angry* is the word that Victor was thinking of, you're ready for more telepathy. Turn to Adele. "Let's try again. Adele, would you please think of a different word that ends in G-R-Y." If she can't think of a word, call it quits and go into a different trick. Chances are, however, that she will think of one. And the only possibility is *hungry*.

Easy Mesmerization

This wonderful old trick never fails to puzzle and entertain. I recommend that you never do it for just one person. You need a group of at least five; in this instance, the larger the audience, the better the trick.

"Ladies and gentlemen, I'd like to try an experiment in mass hypnosis. For this, I'll need everyone's cooperation. As we proceed, you must use the first thing that pops into your head." You proceed with an old number trick. Give the following directions, pausing as necessary: "I would like everyone to think of a number from one to ten. Please double your number. Take that result and add eight to it. Take the result and divide it by two. Now subtract your original number."

Everyone ends up with the number four. (To force a different number, you simply add in double the number you want to force—to force three, for instance, you would have them add in six, rather than eight.)

"Now everyone has a number. I would like each of you to convert your number to a letter of the alphabet. For example, if

your number is one, think of the first letter of the alphabet, A. If
your number is five, think of the fifth letter of the alphabet, E."
Pause. "Everyone should now have a letter in mind."

Everyone should be thinking of the letter D.

"Now I would like you all to think of a country that begins
with the letter you're thinking of. Got one? Good. Everyone
please remember the name of that country.

"Remember that letter you thought of? I'd like you to move to
one letter beyond that one. For example, if you thought of the
letter G, I want you now to think of the letter H. If you thought
of B, you would now think of C. Everyone got the letter? Good.
Now think of an animal whose name begins with that letter."
Pause. "You all should have a country and an animal. Next,
please think of the color of that animal." Pause. "So far you have
a country, an animal, and a color, right? Please concentrate on
all three."

Think briefly, and then shake your head. "Wait a minute.
Something's wrong here. I'm getting the same vibrations from a
lot of you. No, no, no—it's impossible! *There are no grey ele-
phants in Denmark.*"

Take a little bow, so that you get the applause you deserve.
That's right—the vast majority of the group will be thinking,
"Denmark, elephant, grey."

Basic Geometry

You will need two sheets of paper and two pens for this quickie.

"Most attempts at telepathy fail. This is certainly true in my
case. But sometimes I have moderate success. Veronica, will you
assist me?" She will.

"Veronica, I'm sure you're familiar with geometric shapes,
like squares, parallelograms, and so forth. I'd like you to take a
pen and paper and go into the next room. Then draw on the
paper a geometric shape. And inside it, draw another geometric

shape." If Veronica doesn't quite understand what you're talking about, turn over the job to someone else. In this example, she understands perfectly.

While she is gone, you take the other pen and paper and draw a circle with a triangle inside (Illus. 39). Turn the paper over. When Veronica returns, say, "On the other side of this sheet, I have tried to duplicate the figures that you've drawn. My vision of what you were drawing was a little obscure, however. So I'm not sure I got it exactly right. Please show us what you drew."

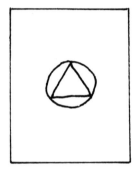

Illus. 39

Chances are very strong that she drew the same thing you did. If she did, hold up your drawing and say, "I *did* get it. My goodness, that's the first time this has happened to me." No one will believe you, of course.

If she did not draw a circle with a triangle inside, you probably have one of the two figures she did draw. When this happens, show your drawing and say, "Yes, it was a little obscure. But I *did* see the circle (whatever) quite clearly."

If you have neither of the figures, show your drawing and say, "Yes, I thought so. My mental picture was really fuzzy. Let's try something else."

Proceed with a surefire mental trick.

Two-Way Prediction

You can correctly predict the result whenever there are two possibilities. For instance, you can predict the winner of any contest between two teams, or between two individuals. Let us assume that you have gathered several persons to watch a boxing match on television. The fight is supposed to be a close one, so you have no particular odds in your favor when you make your prediction. When your guests arrive, indicate an envelope which you have placed in plain sight on a table. At the conclusion of the match, you pick up the envelope and cut off one end. A guest takes the envelope and removes the prediction, which clearly states who the winner will be.

You will need a standard small envelope, approximately 3⅝ inches by 6½ inches, generally referred to as a #6¾ envelope. You will also need a 4-inch by 6-inch file card. Carefully cut off ½ inch from the long side of the file card. Now the card will fit quite nicely inside the envelope.

Let's assume that the big fight is between Murphy and Denton. Using a ruler, draw a light pencil line 1¼ inches from each end of the card. About a quarter inch above the top pencilled line, print this:

Murphy will be

About a quarter inch below the bottom pencilled line, print this:

will be Denton

In the middle of the card, print this in large letters:

THE WINNER

MURPHY WILL BE

THE WINNER

Illus. 40

WILL BE DENTON

The card should look like Illus. 40.

Erase the light pencil lines and place your prediction inside the envelope. Seal the envelope. Eventually, you are going to cut off one end of the envelope. You should cut exactly 1¼ inches from the end. So, ahead of time, place the envelope on the table flap side down. Using your ruler, place a small pencil dot on both sides, 1¼ inches from each end. Thus, when you cut across either end of the envelope, you can go from dot to dot, cutting off precisely 1¼ inches.

You must also remember which end is which. The two names are Denton and Murphy. I place an additional pencil dot at the end where the name Denton is on the prediction. I *know* I'll remember the alphabet, so I place the dot above the name which begins with the earlier letter in the alphabet. Obviously, D comes before M, so I mark the "Denton" end of the envelope.

The prediction is on the table, and a pair of scissors rests near it. The fight is over. "Let's take a look at my prediction," you say. You walk to the table and pick up the envelope with your left hand and the scissors with the right hand. Make sure, when you pick up the envelope, that the winner's name is under your left thumb.

Leaning over the table, place the scissors on one pencil dot and cut across past the other. Let the 1¼-inch piece fall to the table. Place the scissors on the table and pick up the piece with your right hand. With your left hand, give the envelope to one of your friends, saying, "See what my prediction says."

As your friend removes the prediction from the envelope, stick the 1¼-inch piece into your pocket. "Please hold it up so that everyone can see it," you say. As your friend does so, you casually remove the 1¼ inch piece from your pocket and toss it onto the table. Presumably.

Actually, you little rascal, you previously placed a blank cut-down file card inside an envelope, which you sealed. Here's the preparation: Hold the envelope so that the sealed side is towards you and on the upper side. Cut off a 1¼-inch section from each end. The section on your left, you place in your left pocket. The section on your right, you place in your right pocket. Discard the rest of the envelope.

When you cut off the 1¼-inch section from your prediction envelope, you place it into the pocket where a matching section rests. While spectators look at your prediction, bring out the bogus section and toss it onto the table. Thus, if the group eventually gets curious about the narrow section, they will find that the card is blank, and that the narrow section matches perfectly the card and envelope they hold.

ABOUT THE AUTHOR

Bob Longe, a retired English teacher, is an ardent hobbyist. He has charted stocks, played duplicate bridge, and painted. He plays the piano, the tenor banjo, and the ukulele. Inspired by the big stage shows of the great illusionists Blackstone and Dante, he took up magic in the 1930s. He wrote two booklets on card tricks: *The Invisible Deck* was published by the Ireland Magic Company of Chicago; *The Visible Deck* was self-published. Over the years, he has taught magic, particularly card tricks and coin tricks, to dozens of aspiring magicians.

In the late 1970s, Bob wrote, coproduced, and performed in the syndicated radio satire show "Steve Sado, Private Eye." He lives in Rochester Hills, Michigan, with his wife, Betty.

MASTERY LEVELS CHART & INDEX

TRICK	PAGE	DIFFICULTY		
		EASY	HARDER	ADVANCED
Piles of Magic	19		✻	
Power of Three	11		✻	
Power of Seven	33	✻		
Predicting on the Square	51	✻		
Prediction by Hand	84	✻		
Probably Hungry or Angry	87	✻		
Random Choice	55		✻	
Screwball Clock	80	✻		
See My Fist?	9	✻		
Simple Addition	32	✻		
Sky's the Limit	45		✻	
Stacked Dice	29	✻		
Table Tells	43	✻		
Two-Way Prediction	91			✻
Win by a Nose	8	✻		